WILD BILL

Wild Bill

by
Bill Monteith

Praise
BOOKS
Tulsa, Oklahoma

Wild Bill
ISBN 0-89274-324-7
Copyright © 1984 by Bill Monteith
1958 Woodworth Road
Anaheim, California 92804
Published by Praise Books
P.O. Box 35035
Tulsa, Oklahoma 74153

Dedication

To the ones I love the most:

Mavis Shames Monteith

Jeffrey Troy Monteith
Cynthia Dobrenan Monteith
Jill Melissa Monteith
Emily Anne Monteith

Steve Douglas Monteith
Camille Gossman Monteith
Amy Nicole Monteith
Robert Steven Monteith

Louis St. Clair Monteith
Cheryl Cerny Monteith

Contents

1
A Bag Full of Holes

Life for me consisted of amassing a big bag of treasures. I fought and clawed my way up the ladder of success, pausing on each rung to fill my bag with loot. At age forty-four, my whole life was in that bag. But when I got to the top and reached in to claim my treasures, all I had was a bag full of holes.

The water on San Francisco Bay shimmered in the moonlight as our boat plowed through the light chop raised by the gentle breeze of a romantic summer's evening. The strains of the Big Band abroad wafted across the bay as couples danced or lingered over a drink from the open bar.

Earlier that evening we had taken a boat over to Tiburon, passing by Alcatraz on the way. At Tiburon we had eaten dinner, taking up most of the restaurant dining area. It was a beautiful setting in the water at the end of one of the keys. When we returned to San Francisco we would all go back to the presidential suite atop the Fairmont Hotel, where the bar was open for nightcaps and waiters were on hand to serve us.

These were the times I enjoyed most as vice-president of one of the largest construction and financial companies in California, and at that time one of the largest in the world. I enjoyed being able to take clients and potential clients out for a special evening during our conventions, and it gave me a sense of power to be able to pick up the tab for as many as eighty people.

I had started with the company when it was very small: I think I was about the sixth (and youngest) employee to be added to the company payroll. As the firm grew, I grew with it. At the beginning I accompanied the president to look over land for purchase for our subdivisions, but soon I was making those decisions on my own. Then others were hired to work under me and I no longer went out to see land: instead I spent all my time in negotiations with landowners, in the selection of builders, and in taking the property all the way through escrow and transfer of title. At this point, plans would be all drawn up and construction ready to commence, so I would hand the project over to someone else for completion and I would begin the process all over again with a new piece of land.

I did a great deal of entertaining in those days, and was continually wining and dining. In only three or four years our company had grown from a small operation with one secretary to a large concern with many employees. By then we occupied a seven-story building in South Orange County which we had gutted and refurbished as our corporate headquarters.

I clambered my way up the ladder of success by cheating, lying, telling stories about some people and trampling on others, until I reached the top. As vice-president I had offices in five different cities from San Francisco to San Diego and was personally in charge of sixty-five subdivisions, each consisting of a hundred or more houses. Along with my position went everything a man could want—beautiful home, luxury car, large expense account and the excuses to get out of town that all good drunks need.

Yes, that's right. Despite being a success in the business world, Bill Monteith was a drunk. For twenty-two years I staggered all around Orange County. Before the Lord reached His hand down out of heaven and touched me I was known as Wild Bill, the Santa Ana Thrill. I screamed and hollered, fussed and fought, lied and cheated and did everything a human being could do to degrade himself.

The Bible talks about a tremendously successful man called Naaman who was captain of the armies of the king of Syria. He had just one problem to tarnish his success; he was a leper. And as the disease took hold of him, nothing else mattered. Until God delivered him from his affliction, it undermined everything that he ever accomplished.

That's what my life was like as a drunk. Finally, drinking destroyed almost everything I had studied for, fought for, worked for, even cheated for. Then God delivered me and turned my life around.

While I was growing up, my mother and father were both addicted to the bottle. Before my father died he dropped from 260 pounds to 137. So many things ailed him as a result of his drinking that when he died there was not enough room on the death certificate to write them all.

It wasn't that my mother and father didn't love me or were unkind to me, it was just that our house centered around booze. Unlike most people, my childhood memories aren't of family outings, picnics and fun times. They are mostly of picking up drunks—friends of my mother and father—and laying them out on our couches.

Seared indelibly on my mind are incidents such as the one that occurred on my eleventh birthday. My father chased my mother around the kitchen table with a butcher knife in his hand, screaming every obscenity a man has ever uttered, while my sister and I huddled together in a corner, crying our hearts out.

When I reached seventeen World War II was in full swing, so I went into the Navy. There were fifteen hundred men on our ship and most of them were big and tough. I got a view of the Navy different from that of the admiral. Homosexuality and bestiality were rampant, along with every other kind of perversion. They were just as prevalent then as they are today, just less out in the open. Life in the Navy was a daily struggle for survival, so in order to defend myself I learned to box.

I not only became a good fighter, I became a good drinker. If the other branches of the armed forces were anything like the Navy, I don't know how America ever won the war because it seemed that we sailors were drinking constantly while I was in the service. Even in the thick of battle we were pretty well soused. We drank the ''raisin jack'' we kept stored away in the hold of the ship.

Many years after the war, I had the occasion to go back to the Philippines. En route from Guam to Manila aboard a Pan Am jet, our flight captain began to tell the passengers about World War II. As we flew over the Gulf of Leyte, I looked down on the sea in which my ship had sunk when it was hit by a Japanese Kamikase pilot.

After the loss of our ship we spent a long time in the water. It was a living hell. When we were finally rescued we were taken to a hospital in Guam. The Japanese were still in the area, so we were issued sidearms. The enemy would capture the hospital, then we would take it back. When it was all over, only 258 of the 1,500 men aboard our ship had lived to tell the story.

When I returned to my home town I was welcomed as a hero—an eighteen year old who had been in five major battles in the Pacific. My uniform shone with three rows of ribbons across the chest. I received a Presidential Citation, two Letters of Commendation, and a Purple Heart with Cluster. And what do people do with heroes? They wine and dine them, of course.

The war opened a door for me that would never have been possible under normal circumstances. I was given the opportunity to attend the University of Southern California—my dream school. I looked upon it as the finest university in America.

I was doing a lot of social drinking in those days and I thought I could really hold my liquor. I also had an inner sense of pride: "Just imagine, me, a kid who had nothing, and now I'm going to the finest school in the country!"

At USC I rubbed shoulders with the sons and daughters of some of the world's richest families. In fact, John Deere IV of the John Deere Tractor Company flew out to California to attend my wedding a year after graduation. There were a great many wealthy people at USC in those days and it was a real privilege for me to be able to attend. I hardly had two nickels to rub together. In the absence of wealth I worked hard and singled out the moneyed as my friends. As I angled myself in with the rich, I learned to desire the things they enjoyed.

It was at USC that I got to know Mavis, my future wife. We both came from North Hollywood and had gone to the same high school, but I didn't know her in those days. She was three and a half years younger than I, and in high school that was quite a gap. I knew her brother Bob well and had been to their home. But when I returned from the service Mavis had grown up and we found ourselves in the same "year" in college.

It wasn't until our junior year that I got to know her well. By that time we had both become very active in the political and social life of the university. I was president of my fraternity and Mavis was involved in her sorority. Being a natural leader, she later became Panhellenic President. We both served on the school senate.

I was instantly attracted to Mavis. She was about five-eight, slim, with blond hair and blue eyes. I must admit, I liked the packaging, and the contents. Mavis lived in her sorority house on a street called The Row. It was perfectly safe for her to walk alone, but I liked to meet her after her last class of the day and carry her books for her. I think she must have felt as if I followed her all over campus!

Mavis didn't like me at first. I really don't understand why not—after all, I was six feet tall, dark, slim, handsome and witty! She tried to get rid of me, much to my dismay; but her roommate finally talked her into going out with me. One of my Navy buddies was boxing and I really wanted to see him, so our first date was at the ringside. Now Mavis can't stand violence of any kind, so my choice of entertainment wasn't a hit with her—but she did accept a second date. After our first date I told her to cancel all future dates with other guys because I wanted her to go out exclusively with me from then on. We were "pinned" for a year, engaged for another year, and then married in 1951, just one year after graduation.

As a USC graduate I was determined to set the world on its ear. I wanted to prove that I was the smartest young man ever to come out of North Hollywood High School, and I planned to become the richest. My childhood memories ought to have given me enough warning to prevent falling into the same trap as my parents, but they didn't. Somewhere in those years of heavy drinking and wasteful spending in the business world I crossed that fine, invisible line that separates a heavy social drinker from a drunk. Alcohol had been such a way of life in my formative years that I assumed everybody drank, so it was natural for me to gravitate to people who were heavy social drinkers. Every business contact I made was in a bar; I didn't know business could be done in any other place.

My superior was also one of my best friends. We spent a lot of time together in bars, and I used to bail him out of jail. But on December 10, 1970, he fired me.

I couldn't believe it. That night I got a three-week head start on my New Year's hangover. When I woke up, my head was pounding so heavily I could barely stand it. But it was the last time that Wild Bill Monteith ever went to bed with booze in his body.

I had no job, and as the word got around that I had been fired I soon discovered that I had no friends. Nobody called me, and nobody would answer when I called. I found myself in the condition described in Haggai 1:6: ''Ye have sown much, and bring in little; ye eat, but ye have not enough; ye drink, but ye are not filled with drink; ye clothe you, but there is none warm; and he that earneth wages earneth wages to put into a bag with holes.''

That was my life—a bag full of holes.

Climbing the social ladder had never been a truly satisfying experience. I remember the first time that Mavis and I went to an annual conference of builders. Everybody was dressed formally but us. Mavis was about the only lady there who didn't have on a long gown. We were on the first rung of the ladder of success at that time, and we both felt self-conscious because we couldn't afford a beautiful formal for her.

But the following year Mavis had a lovely evening gown made for the occasion. That make her feel better, and I was proud of being able to buy it for her. But now we noticed that all the other women had mink coats. They also arrived in luxury cars and we didn't have a luxury car.

The third year Mavis had a formal, a mink coat, and we had a luxury car. But the evening was still not a success for us because the other wives were loaded with jewelry.

Well, by the fourth year Mavis had a formal, a mink coat, a luxury car, and jewelry. But we still weren't satisfied. Even though we could afford to go to fancy weekend resorts where we could play golf, lounge around the swimming pool, relax in a luxurious whirlpool bath, and be pampered by groomed attendants, we weren't happy with it all. We were living just one show after another, impressing and being impressed.

I remember one several-thousand-dollar, all-night affair we attended at Caesar's Palace in Las Vegas. It was just like those shown in the movies. Our party's private dining room was a replica of Caesar's palace in ancient Rome. The dishes were some of the most beautiful we had ever seen; the table was adorned with highly polished silverware. The waiters and waitresses were clad in togas, and there seemed to be one for every person present. We dined in the sumptuous style of the ancient Romans.

What a letdown it was to go back to our hotel room! We still had to face ourselves. The escape from reality came to an end, as it always did. Then followed the arguments, and the morning-after hangovers.

I wasn't particularly wealthy in those days; it was mostly other people's money I was spending. But I could almost feel what it would be like to be a millionaire some day. Rubbing elbows with the very rich encouraged me to fantasize about my own success. The more I mixed with such people, the more I craved their wealth. I determined to take additional real estate courses, attend more self-help and success seminars, and work harder.

It was enjoyable to spend other people's money because I got the credit for it. People thought it was partly my money too. I suppose I was attempting to gain greatness by association. It felt pretty good to be able to tip a maitre d' $20 (instead of the usual $5) in order to get a good table. It made me a big shot in the eyes of the one I was tipping and the people with me. My ego was boosted every time a wine steward with a large silver medallion around his neck bowed before me. Mavis and I felt like a king and his queen. We really felt that we were someone when we could order the finest wines from the wine cellar, drink expensive bourbon and Scotch whiskey, and eat in restaurants so costly there wasn't even a menu.

But within ourselves we were empty. Pretense isn't very satisfying, and fantasy doesn't endure. And now it was all over: I had been fired! I saw my life as an empty shell, and I didn't know where to turn to fill it with meaning.

At the time I lost my job, Mavis and I were attending a Baptist church. Church attendance seemed like a good social thing for a person who really wanted to get somewhere in this world. The morning after my firing was Saturday and the church was having a work party; we were in a building program to add a gymnasium and kitchen next to our sanctuary.

I climbed onto the roof where the pastor was working and poured out my heart to him, telling him how I had been fired.

"Preacher, what's wrong with me?" I asked. "Look at those people down there with saws, hammers, nails in their hands. Everybody is running around having a good time. Why don't I have the joy and the peace all these other men seem to have? With my ambition to be successful and to move up in the business world, I have always pushed people out of my way, but these guys love one another. They're always smiling. They even enjoy what they're doing. What's wrong with me?"

The pastor pulled a Bible out of his back pocket and told me to turn to Romans 10:9,10. I was so ignorant of the Bible I thought it was in alphabetical order, so when it flipped open to Revelation I found myself searching in blank pages at the back of the book for Romans. When I finally found the passage, I read: "That if thou shalt confess with thy mouth the Lord Jesus, and shalt believe in thine heart that God hath raised him from the dead, thou shalt be saved. For with the heart man believeth unto righteousness; and with the mouth confession is made unto salvation."

I said, "Preacher, is that all there is to it?"

"That's all there is to it, Wild Bill—believe and confess."

"Preacher, I want to believe."

"Let's kneel right here on this roof," he suggested. So right there on that Baptist church roof we knelt in prayer. First he prayed, then I prayed. I had never talked to God before in my life because I had always taken care of everything for myself—I was the "self-made man" type. So I prayed the only prayer I knew: "Now I lay me down to sleep, I pray the Lord my soul to keep."

The preacher was touched by my feeble efforts to reach out to God. Tears began to flood his eyes. Then he prayed again. When he had finished, I began to pray. This time I was able to confess everything I had ever done. I was so hardened physically, mentally, and emotionally that nobody had ever been able to get to me; nobody had been able to make me cry. But now tears of joy began to well up in my eyes and flow down my cheeks.

When the tears were gone I stood up, and in that very moment the Holy Spirit descended upon me and wrapped me in a mantle of love. From that day forward I have been a blood-washed, heaven-bound child of God. Hallelujah!

A couple of months went by. Then one day I was taking a client out to lunch in a restaurant in Orange County. In order to get to the dining area we had to pass through the bar. As we crossed through the bar I heard someone yell, "Hey, Wild Bill!" I peered through the semi-darkness and saw two of my former buddies sitting in a corner, holding liquor glasses, smoke from their ashtrays floating up in front of them.

Two young, heavily made-up girls (who were definitely not their wives) sat with them. They motioned for me to come over.

"Wild Bill, where have you been?" they inquired.

"I've been walking with the Lord."

"Why don't you sit down and have a drink for old times' sake?" they urged.

I looked down at their booze-bloated faces and their red-rimmed, bleary eyes, and tears began to roll down my cheeks.

"Fellows, I can't," I told them. "Because of Calvary, I don't live here anymore." With that I turned and walked away.

During those first months of my new life there were moments when the devil taunted me. Mavis had to be admitted to the hospital three times in one year and didn't seem to be able to shake what was ailing her. (In those days I didn't know about God's power to heal.) Our house was broken into twice within a period of twelve months.

The devil whispered in my ear, "See, Wild Bill, when you were with me you had a long, fancy car; now look at the clunker you're driving. And you had those snappy suits. Now look at the worn threads you have on. You went to all those nightclubs where people respected you and said, 'Mr. Monteith, we have two seats right down front.' Now the best you can afford is a rear booth at McDonald's. You used to have your hair styled; now look at you, going to the barber college!"

One day I decided I had had enough of the devil's taunts, so I climbed into my "clunker" and drove over to the Baptist church where I was saved. I pulled into the parking lot, threw down my anchor, and jumped out. I grabbed a ladder and climbed up onto the roof where I had knelt with the pastor. Removing a pen from my pocket, I sat on that roof and wrote on the side of a three-foot parapet: "Wild Bill Monteith was saved here December 11, 1970."

The devil used to say to me, "You ain't saved, Wild Bill." (I always know when it's the devil talking to me because he can't even speak correct English.) So every time he threw that accusation at me to scare me, I fired up my automobile and drove to the church parking lot to look up at what I had written on the wall.

Today I no longer need to go into the parking lot. I simply drive my *new* automobile past the church and say "Glory, hallelujah!" Now I have an inner awareness of the statement found in 1 John 4:4: ". . . greater is he that is in you, than he that is in the world." What I confessed with my mouth and wrote on that wall has become a living reality to me. I drove down my stake and from that time on nothing could move me. (Even Jesus had to drive down His stake, going back to the place where He was first filled with the Spirit: "And He (Jesus) went away again beyond Jordan into the place where John at first baptized; and there he abode" (John 10:40).)

I know what it is to be a drunk, and I know what it is to be delivered. That's why I have great compassion for all who are hooked on alcohol. I can't turn a blind eye to them as if they didn't exist; I can't ignore their plight. They are human beings with the same potential that you and I have as individuals who have been created in the image of God.

We all have testimonies. Perhaps you have never been in the gutter, so you can't really relate to a drunk as I can. But there are other people you can relate to in a way I can't. You have a testimony that can touch a certain kind of life in a special way.

Perhaps you have always been a good church member, but haven't always known Jesus as your own personal Savior. There are a lot of beautiful people in our churches today who have been baking brownies and filling pews for the last forty years, but who don't know Jesus. If you too have been ''a good church member'' all your life, you can relate to such people. Because my background is different from theirs, we may not be on the same wave length; but you can communicate with them.

I have found that there is no situation that God puts me into that isn't loaded with possibilities for sharing the good news about Jesus. It's a question of knowing how to spot the people who are ready to hear—and a matter of tuning in to the voice of the Spirit in order to act according to His prompting.

I want to share with you how God has used my testimony to touch countless lives. As I do so, I believe you will see how rich with opportunities the everyday, ordinary situations of your own life are for sharing the Good News.

2
That's the Name

When it comes to telling people about Jesus, my greatest burden and success has been with drunks. Wherever I go, God brings them across my path. Everyone has some particular type person he relates to best because every one of us has his own individual story to tell. But many of us have never realized how limitless are the opportunities to share the name of Jesus.

"Mister, I'm cold and hungry."

It was springtime in the state of Washington. "Wild Bill, you come up here in the springtime and you're going to have a good time," I had been promised by the brothers who invited me. "It will be good weather," they guaranteed.

It was beautifully green when I arrived, but it was only a few degrees above zero. I spoke in five cities. On my last morning in Spokane I arose to discover that it was snowing. The temperature had fallen to minus five, and to my California skin it felt like the middle of winter!

I like to walk and talk with the Lord, so I dressed in my warmest clothing and set out across the bridge spanning the Spokane River. After singing the song "Come to the Water," I began to pray in the Spirit. As I paused on the bridge a hand reached out and grasped my shoulder.

I turned to see the man who had accosted me. He was clad in a T-shirt and a pair of pants with a rope for a belt; on his feet were a pair of tennis shoes, but no socks. He looked blue with cold. For some reason, his awkward plea for help irritated me.

"Why don't you go to the YMCA over there?" I suggested, pulling my arm free from his grasp. I began to pray in the Spirit again, but a moment later I felt another tug.

"Mister, I'm cold and hungry," he repeated.

Suddenly, as I peered through the heavy snow-flakes I saw that he looked exactly like my dad. His eyes were sunken into their sockets, and his face was yellow with the pallor of a person as near death as I had ever seen. He reeked of booze. I realized that he was in the last stages of alcoholism. As compassion for him welled up within me, I asked him, "What do you want?"

"I want something to eat."

"Okay, let's go get something."

As we walked across the footbridge, I discovered that his name was Chauncey.

"I'll buy you something to eat," I told him, "but I'm not going to give you any money other than that."

When we had found a diner, he asked for a bowl of soup. As he ate he sounded louder than the Spokane River. After awhile I understood the reason: he had no teeth. Three bowls of soup later, I asked him, "How old are you?"

"I'm seventy," he told me.

"Chauncey," I said, "I've been exactly where you are. I've sat on the same bar stool, drunk the same rot-gut you're drinking. Wouldn't you rather drink some Living Water?

"You go into churches and sleep at night, until some caretaker comes and runs you out in the morning. You wander around in confusion and misery. You've lost your wife, your family, and you've been through all kinds of terrible things. You even almost lost your life.

"I know what it's like, Chauncey. I've had my stomach pumped out, been in beer fights and brawls, been stopped by the police and thrown in the drunk tank. I've done everything you've done, except that today I'm sitting at the feet of God and you're still on the bar stool. That's the only difference between us."

He was listening intently, so I told him what the Bible says in Romans 10:9,10. I explained that God's arms weren't too short to save him. Then I asked him, "Don't you want to accept Jesus?"

"What have I got to lose?" he replied. So then and there we knelt down and prayed. I clasped his skinny little hands and led him in the sinner's prayer. When I looked up again he was weeping.

"Wild Bill," he sobbed, "I'm seventy years old— and you're the first person who has ever talked to me about Jesus. What would have happened if somebody had told me about Him when I was a young boy? Wouldn't my life have been different? I've bummed around every city in the world. I've lost wives and done all sorts of terrible things. My life's a waste."

"No, it isn't," I said, "God promises that at the end of our lives He'll give us twice the blessings as at the beginning. Chauncey, I want you to do something for me."

Reaching into my pocket, I pulled out some money. "I want you to go out and buy something for yourself. You must have gone window shopping many times. Well, I want you to buy something for yourself—something to eat, a fishing rod, an overcoat, whatever you would really like to have. Will you do that for me?"

Chauncey nodded a grateful assent and went on his way. After he had walked out, a waitress came up to me and asked, "Mister, where's your friend?"

"What friend?" I responded.

"You know, that dirty old drunk that was just sitting here."

"Sister," I replied, "that wasn't my friend. That was my brother."

Jesus said, "For I was an hungered, and ye gave me meat: I was thirsty, and ye gave me drink: I was a stranger, and ye took me in: naked, and ye clothed me: I was sick, and ye visited me: I was in prison, and ye came unto me . . . . Verily I say unto you, Inasmuch as ye have done it unto one of the least of these my brethren, ye have done it unto me" (Matt. 25:35-40).

You will encounter people every day of your life who need to know Jesus—at your place of work, in school, in your social or civic club, at the supermarket, wherever you go. There may be someone you see every day who doesn't know about Jesus—who has never heard how He came to change lives and how He can change their life if they will only allow Him to. How will you feel on the Day of Judgment as you stand with Jesus and watch that person you neglected pass by, never having been saved? you could have told him or her about the Lord Jesus, but you didn't. How will you feel when he or she looks you in the eye and you remember all the times you might have said something but didn't?

Most people have heard of Jesus at least, even though they may not know that He is alive and willing to save them. But when I was in Australia I met a man who had never heard the name of Jesus.

It was late at night as I rounded a corner and

almost tripped over a drunk who was lying in the doorway of the Adelaide Hotel, clutching a bottle of muscatel. He had obviously thrown up all over himself and was a disgusting sight to behold—and smell. The people I was with took a long turn around him and went on into the hotel.

I was sharing a room with my friend Willie Murphy, the black evangelist. I took the elevator and arrived at the door of our third-floor room. I tried to insert my key into the lock, but it wouldn't fit. I wondered what on earth was going on. Suddenly I heard the Lord say, "Wild Bill, I thought I brought you to Australia to minister to everybody."

"Come on, Lord, it's late at night. I *have* ministered to everybody," I answered. "Who was the only guy who put a Gospel tract in the taxi cab when he gave the driver a tip? When we registered in the hotel, who said 'Praise the Lord' to the girl at the desk and told her what we were doing while he handed her one of those 'Thank you for your service' cards? Me! Did the other guys do that? Not one of them. None of the seventeen did a thing. They all went back to their rooms because they were tired. And the man who brought me my ice water—didn't I give him a *Voice* magazine with my testimony in it?"

I put the key back into the lock. I could hear the television playing inside the room and Willie singing along with it. (Sometimes at night when he was lying in bed, Willie would have headphones on and I would think he had fallen asleep, but suddenly he would startle me by starting to sing.) I wanted to get in that room badly; I told myself how neat it would be to have some fellowship together with Willie. But the key would not work.

"Okay, Lord," I finally broke down and asked, "who did I miss?"

"The drunk in the doorway," the Lord answered.

"Come on Lord," I protested, "that's one guy I'm not going to minister to. He's bombed, he's sick, and he's passed out. He's too drunk to accept any ministry."

Though the key had worked perfectly before, there was no way I could get it to fit our room lock. I worked and worked, but to no avail.

"All right, I'll do it," I said with resignation, "but under protest."

I really didn't feel like going back down to the street to talk to someone who was unconscious, so on my way down I picked up an ice bucket and filled it with water, carting it through the lobby with me. I knew that people were saying, "There goes one of those dumb Yanks again."

"He's going to be gone," I told myself. "I know he's going to be gone." But when I turned the corner, there he was, lying in the same position, bottle still in hand. I picked up that bottle and threw it into the litter basket, then I tossed the entire contents of the ice bucket over him. He didn't bat an eyelid; he was as stiff as a board.

"Well, Lord," I said, "if You want me to preach to him, I'll preach to him." I knelt down beside him, took my Bible in hand and began to give the unconscious man my testimony.

"Brother," I said, "I don't know who you are or what you're doing in this doorway. Man, I've been in many of these. I've passed out in doorways and alleys. I've awakened many times with the sun coming up over the mountains and found myself in my car in some strange city. I've had my stomach pumped and been in drunk tanks. Brother, I've done everything you've done. I know your spirit can hear me, so I'm going to tell you about Somebody you probably don't know about. His name is Jesus.''

I turned to the book of Romans and read my favorite passage. Then I related all of the wonderful blessings the Lord had bestowed upon me after He had raised me up out of the gutter and set my feet on the solid rock of Jesus.

By now I was having a good time and hardly noticed the people who walked in a large arc around me, glancing back over their shoulders at the ''crazy Yank.'' I didn't care what they thought or said because I was preaching the Word of God. I began to pray with the drunk and went through the sinner's prayer with him. When I was through I stuffed a card in his pocket on which I had scribbled, ''Meet me tonight at seven o'clock at Apollo Stadium; I want to introduce you to someone.''

When I got back up to my room, I inserted the key and, sure enough, it unlocked! Willie was fast asleep so I didn't turn on the light. As I came out of the bathroom I sneaked over to my bed in the dark and hopped in. When my head hit the pillow it contacted something furry. I jumped out of bed, groped for the light switch, bumping my toe on the night stand as I did, and finally located my glasses. I looked down at the pillow. Did spiders really come that big in Australia? Then I realized that Willie had left his black Afro hairpiece on my pillow!

The following evening I was in charge of the preliminary preparations at the stadium. I was busy with my assigned duties when suddenly an usher interrupted me: "Wild Bill, there's a man out here who wants to see you. Do you want to talk to him?"

"Sure, I'll talk to him," I answered glibly. "Who is he?"

"I don't know," he said, "but he knew your name."

The little fellow came up to me. "You Wild Bill?" he asked.

"Yes, that's me."

"Well, here I am. My name's Alf."

I hadn't a clue as to who this man was, until he pulled the card from his pocket.

"It says here to meet you at seven o'clock at Apollo Stadium," he read. "Well, I'm here. You said you'd introduce me to someone."

"Oh, I know you," I said, recognizing him at last.

"Yeah, I'm the drunk," he confessed. "When I woke up at two o'clock this morning I was sober for the first time in a long time and it scared me. I began to go through my pockets and found your card. Then I remembered someone talking to me. He mentioned a name, but I couldn't quite recall it, so I began to go through all the names I could think of. I was very analytical about it. I started with Alf, Allen . . . and went through the whole alphabet. You said a name, but I just couldn't remember it."

I prodded him to remember, but to no avail. He had been so determined to meet me and find out what that name was, he had spent the whole day in the park just waiting for seven o'clock.

As we talked I learned that Alf was from a small town some two hundred miles out of Towoomba in Queensland. When I asked him what he had been doing in Adelaide he pronounced proudly, "I've been drinking all the time." He had been a drunk for seven-teen years.

"Well, at least you're consistent," I told him. "A lot of people are not consistent, even some Christians. At least you do something every day."

"Yes, I sure do," he agreed. "Now, tell me His name."

"Okay. His name is Jesus."

"What was that again?"

"His name is Jesus."

Alf's eyes lit up as he recognized the name from the night before. "That's the name! That's the name!" he cried excitedly. "Who is He?"

"Would you like me to tell you about Jesus?" I suggested.

"That's the name!" he rattled back. "Say it again."

"Jesus."

"That really sounds good. I never heard that name before."

I couldn't believe it. "You're putting me on," I chided.

"Putting you where?" he asked. The man was serious.

"You mean you really have never heard the name of Jesus?" I asked almost incredulously.

"No, I've never heard that name. Say it one more time."

I repeated the name. Every time I mentioned the name of Jesus throughout our conversation, Alf would say, "That's the name!" I could tell it really excited him. "I want to meet Him," he insisted.

I took out my Bible and he asked what it was. He had never seen a Bible in his entire life, he claimed.

"Oh, come on," I chuckled, "Now I know you're putting me on!"

"No, I don't know what it is," he said.

"Don't you have a library in your town?"

"In my *town*?" he laughed. "No, I live out in the bush; there are only aborigines out there. We don't even have a gas station."

There were some Bibles for sale at the book table. I reached over and picked one up. Opening it to the book of Romans, I quoted the ninth verse of the tenth chapter.

"That's all there is to it," I explained. "Wouldn't you like to accept Jesus into your heart? You haven't confessed Him yet but you do believe, don't you?"

"Yes," Alf nodded, "I really believe."

"Well, let's confess Him." We went through the sinner's prayer on our knees, and when we got all the way through he began to weep.

"Am I really saved?" he asked, almost in disbelief at what had happened to him.

"Brother," I confirmed, "you have all the privileges I have. You are a king and a priest, a joint-heir with Jesus. You don't have to sit on a bar stool now, you can stand before the King of Kings where I am. Welcome to the Kingdom! By the way, you can have this Bible, because I want you to go back and tell your whole family about Him."

"Who?" Alf was smiling.

"Jesus," I said.

"That's the name! That's the name!" he exclaimed excitedly, a gleam in his eyes. Perhaps Alf didn't understand much theology, but there was no doubt that Jesus had touched his life by the power of the Holy Spirit.

By this time a crowd of five thousand people was looking at us; the violins were tuning up and the orchestra was in its place. Alf rose from his knees and took about three paces, then turned around, came back, grabbed me by the lapel and said, "Wild Bill, one more time!"

"The name is Jesus," I repeated.

"That's the name!" And with that he set off toward the railing, his Bible under his arm. Springing over the railing, his mouth formed the words, "What's the name?"

I shouted at the top of my voice, "The name is Jesus!"

"Yeah, yeah, yeah!" he shouted, and off he went.

While in Brisbane, Australia, I taped a couple of radio shows. I gave my testimony on the first program and a man named Roderick MacAlpine happened to be listening. He was a drunk; in fact, he had been a drunk longer than I. He had been through the rehabilitation programs and had failed at every one of them. His testimony was that of W. C. Fields: "It's not hard to stop drinking; I've done it a thousand times!"

The first time this man heard me on the radio he said to himself, "I can't believe that guy. How can a drunk change overnight?"

On the second program I told about all the places the Lord had taken me since my conversion, how I had visited ten countries since 1977. I said that except for my service days I probably wouldn't have ever traveled as far as Tijuana had I not become a Christian, but that here I was preaching in Australia. I told how the Lord had provided me opportunities to preach the Gospel in the Middle East, Germany, Yugoslavia, Canada, Guatemala, the Philippines, and many other places.

The programs really seemed to get to Roderick. In reaction against what he was hearing, the evening following the second broadcast Roderick decided to get as drunk as he possibly could. He sat down with a fifth of whiskey and began to drink. But the more he drank, the more sober he became! That really made him mad and he went through his considerable vocabulary of curse words, dredging up every obscenity he could think of. Still, nothing would happen. Finally he grew so disgusted that he said, ''Well, I guess I'll stop drinking.''And he did!

God touched Roderick MacAlpine that night through someone who had lived in the gutter with him. Sometimes it takes a drunk to reach a drunk.

Pastor Rex and his wife were two beautiful people I had the opportunity to spend time with in Australia. We were walking down a street in Brisbane one time when a drunk crashed into me just outside a movie theater. He could barely stand on his feet. Pastor Rex reeled back in disgust. As the man bounced off me, he staggered toward the door of the theater and tried to open it. He was a pitiful sight, his clothes tattered, his hair disheveled, the stench of his unbathed body filling the air.

I walked over to him and asked, ''What are you trying to do?''

''I want to see the show,'' he slurred.

''All right, let's go,'' I said, opening the door to the lobby of the theater and leading him inside. Pastor Rex followed behind us.

When we reached the box office the drunk couldn't find his wallet. "I'll pay for it," I volunteered; it was only $2.50. Taking him on into the theater, I guided him to a seat. On the way out I stopped at the refreshment counter. Handing some money to the lady on duty, I said, "If there's anything he needs—a Coke or some coffee—buy it for him."

As I walked out of the theater Pastor Rex was crying. "What are you crying for?" I asked.

"I've been a pastor for twenty-one years," he sobbed. "When that fellow hit you, I was revolted by the sight of him. It's sickening for me to think of a man so drunk he can't even walk down the street. Then I saw you take him into your heart and show compassion to him. You bought his ticket, put him in his seat, and provided some money so he could have coffee afterwards. I would never have done that."

You have to have been a drunk to know what it's like. I understand those people. For twenty-two years I was one of them.

There is a fine line between being a heavy social drinker and being a drunk. Every year more than 100,000 Americans cross that line. Do you know what that adds up to? More than fourteen million drunks staggering around the United States! One out of every thirteen Americans—men, women, and children—is a drunk.

Of all the deaths on the highway, day and night, 60 percent are caused by drivers who have been drinking. When I say drinking, I mean drunk enough to be locked up for drunken driving. Some 55 percent of the deaths on motorbikes are caused by drinking; and 50 percent of all pedestrians killed each year on our streets and highways are drunk.

Crime in our society is skyrocketing. Seventy-five percent of all the people in our prisons today are there because they committed a crime under the influence of alcohol. The list of crimes caused by alcohol is endless. Child molestation, wife-beatings, suicides, and homocides frequently are caused by drinking.

On any given weekend between 6:00 p.m. Saturday and 4:00 a.m. Sunday, every fourth person in California is so drunk he can't walk straight. A shocking 80 percent of all high school students in the U.S. get bombed over the weekend; they are steady drinkers. In the Santa Ana, California, school system a seven-year-old alcoholic was recently discovered. One day he came to school coughing. The nurses and doctors couldn't understand what was wrong with him. Then it was discovered that he had tequila in his cough medicine. He was totally addicted to it—a confirmed drunk at age seven!

No wonder the Scriptures warn: "Whose heart is filled with anguish and sorrow? Who is always fighting and quarreling? Who is the man with bloodshot eyes and many wounds? It is the one who spends long hours in the taverns, trying out new mixtures. Don't let the sparkle and the smooth taste of strong wine deceive you. For in the end it bites like a poisonous serpent; it stings like an adder. You will see hallucinations and have delirium tremens, and you will say foolish, silly things that would embarrass you no end when sober. You will stagger like a sailor tossed at sea, clinging to a swaying mast. And afterwards you will say, 'I didn't even know it when they beat me up .. Let's go and have another drink!'" (Prov. 23:29-35LB).

What an accurate description of a person whose life has become an endless round of drinking bouts.

Is this what anyone really wants his life to be?

"Wine gives false courage; hard liquor leads to brawls; what fools men are to let it master them, making them reel drunkenly down the street!" (Prov. 20:1 LB). We could add to this thought that drink is the greatest single cause of death and injury on our highways today, because the drunk's false courage leads him to think that he can drive safely. He doesn't realize he is swerving all over the road, endangering his own life as well as the lives of others.

Sometimes a woman will say to me, "Wild Bill, my husband couldn't make the Full Gospel meeting tonight. He's having a bad time. He's throwing up, he's so sick."

"What's wrong?" I ask.

"Oh, he's been drinking. He's gone to various progams, he belongs to AA, he's been to the doctor. But nothing cures him, he's really sick."

I tell them, "No, he's not sick, he's a slave to sin."

Less than ten percent of the drunks who submit themselves to various rehabilitation programs ever fully recover from alcoholism. But in the program called Teen Challenge, more than 80 percent of the alcoholics who participate are delivered. That's because what we commonly call "alcoholism" is really the sin of drunkenness, and Jesus is the only One Who can deliver a person from sin. When listing the works of the flesh, the Bible includes drunkenness right along with adultery, idolatry, witchcraft, heresy and murder. (Gal. 5:19-21.) But if a person confesses his condition and receives Jesus as his personal Savior, he can be delivered.

How tragic, then, that there are Christians who are still slaves to the bottle.

Toni is a thirty-four-year-old bartender. I think she is her own best customer. She once made a decision for Christ, but today she gets so bombed that she doesn't know where she is. She wears a wrist bracelet bearing her name and address so people who find her inebriated can call her mother to come pick her up. She's married, but her husband is as bad as she is.

Toni's problem is that she doesn't really want to stop drinking. One day her mother called me and said, "Wild Bill, I've got Toni over here. I picked her up when someone called and said she didn't know where she was."

I went over to her mother's home and prayed with Toni. As I prayed she began to weep. "Oh, praise God!" her mother exclaimed. "She's back with the Lord!"

But something told me it wasn't genuine. "No, she's conning us," I had to explain to her mother.

One Tuesday evening I went into a bar where I knew I could find Toni. It was wall-to-wall with blue-collar workers. A lot of them were truckers. From the looks of them, it was pretty obvious that when these fellows weren't working they were standing at a bar some place with both fists locked around a beer mug.

"Is Toni here?" I yelled at the top of my voice. Instantly I had everyone's attention. The musical combo stopped playing. Out of the silence a little voice said, "I'm here, Wild Bill." I walked over and looked down at Toni. At thirty-four years of age, she looked seventy. Her face was big and bloated and she was surrounded by guys, most of them smoking pot.

"Toni, your mother tells me you're going to Hawaii tomorrow," I said. "I've come here for two reasons. One of them is as a messenger from Jesus Christ to tell you that right now you can repent of your sins and be delivered from booze.'' She began to cry.

''The other thing I came to say is goodbye. I'm not going to see you anymore, because you're killing yourself.

''Now don't you want to come back with the Lord and be delivered before it's too late for you?''

She looked at me with sad eyes and said, ''I can't.''

''Why can't you?'' I asked. By this time the guys at her table were starting to get their backs up. But it didn't disturb me if they got huffy because I've never been injured yet on an errand for the Lord.

''I'd have to give up too much,'' Toni sobbed.

''What are you going to give up—all these 'friends' here?''

I pointed to her bar stool. ''When I was drinking, that stool was mine. I owned it for the time that I was buying my drinks. The minute I got off it, somebody else sat on it and it was his while he was buying. You don't own anything, not even this stool. You don't even own your own body anymore because you're selling it to booze.''

Toni's self-image was about as low as any I have ever seen. She had no self-worth left. Why else would she, or anyone, do such a thing to herself? I knew that all I could do was give her one thing to hang onto—the fact that I cared about her, no matter how low she sank.

''Do you mind if I pray for you?'' I asked. She said she wanted me to.

Turning to the rest of the people in the bar, I asked them to bow their heads because I was about to pray for Toni. Not one of them refused to bow his head.

I began to call upon God to come in the power of the Holy Spirit and touch that dear little sister. When I had finished praying I told her, "All I want to say is that if you ever need me, if you ever want God in your life, all you have to do is pick up the telephone and call me. I don't care where you are, you can call me collect." She promised she would, and I walked out.

It isn't my responsibility to convict people. That's the work of the Holy Spirit. I don't know if Toni will ever come back to the Lord, but I do know that she knows there is someone who loves her and is ready to help her. All I can do is offer her a helping hand.

If a person who has received Jesus still doesn't know who he is, instead of living like a child of God he will live like a sinner. That was what was taking place in Corinth when Paul wrote his first letter to the church there. They were even getting drunk at the Communion table!

In 1 Corinthians 6 Paul talked about two categories of people: those in the world, and those in the Kingdom of God. There are just these two groups: the saints, and the unrighteous. But the saints in Corinth were living like the unrighteous. They were *not* the unrighteous, they were sinning saints.

"Know ye not that the unrighteous shall not inherit the kingdom of God?" Paul asked them in verse nine. The unrighteous weren't those in the church who were getting drunk and committing sexual immorality. Because a lot of people don't read the passage fully, they think Paul is saying that saints who sin will not inherit the Kingdom. No, that is not his point. We inherit the Kingdom solely by grace, not by works. But Paul is drawing a contrast between the unrighteous of the world and the saints. "How can you live like the unrighteous people of the world,'' he asks, ''when you are no longer such people, but saints?''

No fornicator, adulterer, drunkard or swindler will inherit the Kingdom of God. *But one who has been saved by grace is no longer such a person.* Instead, Paul says of the Corinthians who were still doing some of these things, ''And such were some of you: but ye are washed, but ye are sanctified, but ye are justified in the name of the Lord Jesus Christ, and by the Spirit of our God'' (v. 11).

Paul then goes so far as to say that a Christian who consorts with a prostitute takes Jesus Christ with him as he goes to a house of prostitution. Since in his spirit a Christian is joined to the Lord, he cannot become involved with such immorality without defiling the temple of God. Notice, the Christian doesn't cease to be the temple of God—he defiles what is still the temple in which Christ lives. If he really grasped what he was doing, such activity would be unthinkable to him.

Here, then, is how the person locked into the sin of drunkenness or any other sin may be delivered. He must see that he is a precious, worthy child of God—that Jesus Christ lives in him. When he sees that, he will have a deep and genuine sense of self-esteem, and with that will come the desire to walk worthy of such a high calling. When an individual wants to be the person God re-created him to be, in Christ, the Lord will provide him with the determination to truly become that person. Old things pass away, and all things become new. (2 Cor. 5:17.)

''Oh, I'm so weak, I really *need* a drink,'' many drunks will say to the first person they meet after they have just come off a drying-out program. And there will always be someone there ready to ''lend a helping hand" by providing that drink. So then the "reformed" drunk is soon right back where he started. But when God gives a person a sense of true worth, he has a desire *not* to drink: he *wants* to be delivered. And when a person makes that decision, the fruit of the Holy Spirit will well up within him and provide him the self-control to overcome his weakness.

We will encounter people who are weak and who need to know that they are of value to God. How can we show them that? By showing them by our treatment of them that they have worth. Whether they are unbelievers or backsliders, they need to know that God cares for them. Jesus told the story of the shepherd who left the ninety-nine to go in search of the one lost sheep. Do we care enough to help the one who is lost?

Anyone can condemn. But God didn't call us to condemn people, He called us to show love to them and to reach out a helping hand. When a person is the recipient of genuine love—when he senses that you really care about him—his life may be spared.

One night a woman telephoned me. She sounded frantic. "Wild Bill," she pleaded, "Ben's holed up in a motel down on Main Street with two guns and he's going to kill himself. Can you do something before I call the police?"

I met her at the motel and she pointed to Ben's room. "Are you sure you dare go in there?" she asked.

"Listen," I told her, "nobody can hurt me. God has given His angels charge over me." I opened the door and there was Ben with two guns trained on me.

"I'm going to blast you and blow you to pieces," he threatened.

"Good," I said boldly, "absence from the body is presence with the Lord. Hallelujah!"

"You're not afraid of me, are you?" he asked.

"No, I'm not afraid of you at all," I announced, "because greater is He that is in me than he that is in the world, and I can overcome you, Ben. Now if you'll put down those guns, you and I will talk."

When he realized that I wasn't afraid, he put down the guns and we began to talk. He had been drinking for forty years, and after that long it's not easy to break any habit, much less drinking. But as we began to pray that night, the Spirit of God came down upon us and Ben began to shake and tremble. We shared together all night, then had breakfast together the next morning.

Ben was born again that night. Later he quit his job because of the pressure to drink that was put upon him there. Today he's a child of God. Mavis and I visited with him and his wife recently. God has truly restored the years that the locusts had devoured. He has blessed Ben and his wife's latter years twice as much as their former. They live in a lovely home— one of the most beautiful I have ever seen—on a hillside overlooking Morro Bay. The home contains the finest of everything and features a great deal of hand-crafted custom woodwork which Ben did mainly by himself. It was a delight to see how their lives have changed because they know Jesus today.

I never know how God is going to use me, but every day of our lives Mavis and I expect to touch the lives of others for Jesus. We have a deep compassion for drunks because I know what it's like to be one and Mavis knows what it's like to live with one.

I went to a jail as a result of a telephone call from a woman whose husband had been picked up as a child molester. She was terrified because he was going to be sent to the penitentiary—and you may know what other inmates do to child molesters if they can get their hands on them. Such prisoners are usually kept in a special section with wire around it to protect them from attack. If this man were to go to prison, it was very likely he would end up dead.

He was shaking when I arrived, and I had just twenty minutes to spend with him. So I began with Romans 10:9,10 and told him that if he would be saved God would give him the desires of his heart. "What are your desires?" I asked.

"I don't want to go to prison," he said." I'd rather go to Patton (a rehabilitation center) where I can get well. I want to get well."

I was talking to him through a glass partition by means of a telephone. Although we were physically separated, I was able to lead him to a saving knowledge of the Lord Jesus Christ right there in that jail. I had the witness of the Spirit that it was a good salvation experience, so I said, "We'll kneel in prayer for your desires right now."

When I left the jail I called the man's wife and told her that he had accepted the Lord. "Not only that," I told her, "he's going to go to Patton."

"How do you know?" she inquired.

"The Holy Spirit told me," I said. "The Lord doesn't want him to go to the penitentiary where he would be killed."

Two days later I received a call from Ben's wife telling me that her husband was in Patton. Oh, the power of the name of Jesus! Whether it's a child molester or a drunk who is unconscious in the streets of Adelaide, the name of Jesus is mighty to save and deliver!

Will you tell someone about Jesus today? Share what He has done for you. He'll bring people across your path with whom you can relate, just as He does for me. Whatever their need in life, Jesus is the name that can help them.

3
Heart Trouble

Sometimes it's just too late—a person's heart has hardened to the point of no return. What if someone had reached him just a little sooner, when his heart was still soft? Being a witness for Jesus is a matter of life and death.

A story is told of a little old lady everybody thought was the saint of the town. She gave the impression of being extremely poor. One day she became ill, so ill that she had to be rushed to the county hospital.

"I think there's something wrong with my heart," she told the doctor in attendance.

When he asked her if she had any money to pay for her treatment she told him that she was penniless. He wanted to take an x-ray of her chest, but she refused to remove her clothes. Finally, as a last resort, the doctor had to take the x-ray through her clothing.

While examining the x-ray the doctor noticed a strange image on the negative. Closer inspection revealed that pinned to the little old lady's underclothing was a bag filled with money.

When the doctor went back to her room, the lady asked, "Did you find anything wrong with my heart?"

"I surely did," he replied.

"Can you fix it?" she asked.

"No," confessed the doctor, "there is nothing I can do for you."

"Why, doctor?" she inquired.

"Because your heart is full of lies, trickery and deceit."

There are people whose hearts becomes so hardened that it is impossible to help them. At the airport in Dallas, Texas, while on my way from Amarillo to San Antonio, I was restless. What is there to do in an airport? If you've seen one, you've seen them all, as they say. So, out of sheer boredom, I began to walk up and down the concourse, looking for someone to pass the time of day with. I was ready to talk to anybody who would talk to me—the shoeshine man, the barber, the sky cap.

Coming to a little old man who must have been eighty, I sat down beside him. It was an extremely hot day, but he had on an overcoat and a hat.

"Brother, my name is Wild Bill," I said. "What's yours?"

He told me his name.

"Brother, are you saved?" I asked. (Why beat around the bush? If a person is saved, then we have Jesus to talk about; if not, I have an opportunity to witness.)

"No, Wild Bill, I'm not saved," he answered. "In fact, I can't be saved."

"Well, brother, that seems strange," I replied, "because my Bible tells me in 2 Peter 3:9 that God is not willing that any should perish but that all should come to repentance. And 1 Timothy 2:4 says that God will have all men to be saved."

"No," he said, "not me. I *can't* be saved."

"But I just read you the texts," I persisted. "The Bible says that God is not willing for anyone to perish but wants *all* to be saved."

"Wild Bill, let me tell you something," he answered. "When I was a young boy I lived in the western plains of Texas. I went to one of those old revival meetings where there was sawdust on the floor and a preacher behind the pulpit preaching his lungs out. Suddenly the Spirit of God came down upon me; He even called me by my name. 'Tonight's your night,' He told me. 'You must accept Jesus tonight or you will never be saved.'

"I stood there trembling and had to grab hold of the pew in front of me. As I shook I hollered at the top of my voice, 'No, God, I don't want to be saved!' At that moment the Holy Spirit left me."

The old man rose to his feet, buttoned his overcoat, and began to walk away from me. He had gone about three paces when he turned around and came back to me, tears streaming down his face.

"You know, Wild Bill, He's never been back," he said sorrowfully. Then he turned around and I watched as he shuffled off down the concourse.

I began to weep. "Oh, God," I prayed, "don't let that happen to anybody. Don't let anyone's heart become hardened like that!" Many times at night I awaken and see that little old man in his black overcoat and his little hat, sadly shuffling off into the distance.

The Apostle Paul tells us that the Gospel divides human beings into two camps. "For we are a fragrance of Christ to God among those who are being saved and among those who are perishing," he says, "to the one an aroma from death to death, to the other an aroma from life to life. And who is adequate for these things?" (2 Cor. 2:15-16 NAS).

There is great rejoicing among the angels of heaven when a sinner turns to Jesus, but it is a terribly sad affair when anyone becomes so hardened that he cannot respond. I have shed a lot of tears over people like that. As I watched that little old man walk away, I felt totally inadequate for the job to which God has called me. If only someone, somehow, could have reached him! I ask the Lord continually to make me the most effective witness possible so that I might win those to whom He sends me.

An old friend of mine called me while I was in the East and asked if I would have breakfast with him while I was in town. I agreed, and we set a time and place to meet. The next morning I walked into the restaurant and saw Mike sitting in a window booth with a glass in his hand. It seemed as though every time I saw Mike he had a glass in his hand. My spirit was weeping as I approached him.

Over breakfast I asked him about some old friends from the past.

"How is Bob doing?" I inquired. Bob was president of an eastern bank.

"Oh, he's still swinging with the same stable of girls," Mike retorted. "He's got his boats and his airplanes. He's still lying, cheating, and taking loans underneath the table, like he always did. He's ruthless, cruel—he's broken a lot of people, including John. He's a millionaire several times over, but he's gone through several wives."

"Tell me about Jim," I said. Jim was president of an electrical company.

"He's got the same wife, but she's forty-five and trying to act like she's eighteen—a woman with a child's mind. Her life consists of chasing after tennis pros. Jim feeds his 275 pounds with a diet of bonded booze and platinum blondes. He's a millionaire one day and in court fighting with his creditors the next. He lives in a world of phony money and bouncing checks."

"Well, how's Rick, the president of the plumbing company?" I inquired.

"Oh, he's the same old guy," Mike answered. "He's living in one of those sex communes where everybody shares their wives and all their worldly goods. He's got everything and he's tried everything, but he's still unhappy, forever thinking about sex and suicide. You remember how his body was in such great shape from working out with weights? Well, he can't even pass an insurance physical anymore."

"I know about Dave," I said. "He called me about two years ago when he was in the hospital. He was dying of a cancerous tumor, so I went up to pray with him. As we started to pray I said, 'Dave, the Lord has just told me that you are going to be healed. You're going to go through an operation, but it will be successful. The Lord wants you to give your life to Him.'"

(Dave had always been a member of a liturgical church but had never professed Jesus Christ as his personal Savior. He was faithful to his church, but he didn't know the Lord. When I prayed for him in the hospital that day I asked the Lord to touch his stony heart. While I was in Australia he called Mavis and told her that he had accepted the Lord. Mavis bought him a Bible and took it over to him. His wife and children thought he was crazy, but he was praising the Lord for his healing.)

"And how about you, Mike?" I continued.

"You know, Wild Bill, when you first started out on this religion bit, we all thought you were crazy. We looked on you as one of those religious nuts, a Jesus freak, a weirdo. We couldn't understand your getting out of a business where you were making all that money and having such a good time, like we always did with our long lunch breaks. But we've watched your life these past seven years, and one thing we know is that you're the only one of the whole bunch of us who's really happy. We hear about your being on TV and about your travels all over the world. We're burning the candle at both ends trying to make it pay off just so we can live. You've got the answer. But we can't do what you're doing—because if we gave it all up like you did, we'd be broke, and that scares us."

"Mike, don't you realize that I'm the richest man on earth—a king, a priest, a joint-heir with Jesus? You can have the same thing I have, and it won't cost you a dime."

"I just can't give it up, Wild Bill," he answered.

"Is there anything I can do to explain it to you better than I have, these last seven years?" I inquired. "Obviously I haven't done a very good job of it— you're still outside the Kingdom. Wouldn't you like to accept Jesus as your Savior?"

"Wild Bill, I just can't do it. I have everything I need; I don't want Jesus right now."

I felt tears welling up in my eyes so I bowed my head; I didn't want Mike to see them. He placed an insurance form on the table in front of me. "Here, I want you to sign this," he urged.

"What is it?"

"It's a life insurance policy."

I stared at the form. It was a policy for $300,000 and the premium was $9,000. "Mike, you know I don't have that kind of money," I exclaimed.

"I'm paying it for you," he answered.

"Why are you doing that for me?" I asked in astonishment.

"This is my ace in the hole," he explained. "Maybe somewhere down the line I may need you."

I sensed that Mike was showing a tangible form of respect for all that I stood for, even though he was not willing to pay the price of Christian discipleship himself. And his action was also an answer to prayer. At the time I had no insurance, though I had always carried it in the past.

I just couldn't let him go without making one last effort, "Mike, the Bible says in Romans 13:12 that the night is far spent and the day is at hand." But my words fell on deaf ears. As I signed the form, a tear rolled down my cheek.

Mike rose to his feet, patted me on the shoulder, and said, "Wild Bill, thanks a lot. I'll be seeing you."

I didn't move from the booth after he had left. I had been sharing with these men for seven years, yet only one out of five had found Jesus. "Lord, I don't understand," I said. "Obviously I don't belong in this ministry. If I can't convince my own friends, how can I ever hope to convince anybody else?"

The Lord encouraged me, "Wild Bill, the same thing happened to Me." The Scripture flashed to mind: "And they were offended at him. But Jesus said unto them, A prophet is not without honour, but in his own country, and among his own kin, and in his own house" (Mark 6:3,4).

When the waitress came by to see if I wanted more coffee, I asked her, "Do you know what the saddest words ever written are?" She thought I was a bit weird I'm sure, but she confessed that she didn't know and asked me what they were. I pulled my Bible from my pocket, turned in it to Jeremiah 8:20, and read, "Harvest is past, the summer is ended, and we are not saved."

Walking out to my car, I needed something to reassure me of my calling. Suddenly the Lord gave me 1 Timothy 1:12: "I thank Christ Jesus our Lord, who hath enabled me, for that he counted me faithful, putting me into the ministry."

I have come across a great many people who have hardened their hearts. Sometimes their hardness has been caused by the events of their lives; sometimes it is a result of their own choices. But there is one thing I want to be sure of, and that is that I never contribute to someone else's hardness by the way I conduct myself.

There may be a time in a person's life when he is still "soft" of heart and could be reached by just the right word. A few years later, it could be too late. A kind action, a demonstration of love at the right moment, may make all the difference. Mavis and I go out into the world each day deeply conscious of the fact that we are going to have an impact on every person with whom we come in contact. Each meeting is a divine encounter. We will affect each person's appointment with destiny either positively or negatively; there is no neutral ground. We cannot avoid either helping to save someone or pushing him one step further toward the ultimate tragedy.

Witnessing is serious business. I never want to waste an opportunity, because tomorrow may be too late for that individual. Only *today* do I have an opportunity to be a "savor of life" to other people.

The very first time I spoke at a Full Gospel Business Men's Fellowship chapter meeting was in Capistrano Valley, California. After the meeting a lady came up to me. When she was about ten feet from me, I knew she was drunk; I could smell the alcohol on her. She was around forty, trying to look like eighteen. She had on a mini-skirt, a Shirley Temple wig, about an inch and a half of pancake makeup on her face, and false eyelashes long enough to hang your hat on.

"Wild Bill," she asked, "will you pray for me?"

"Yes, I'll pray for you," I told her. "What's your name?"

"Patty."

At that instant the Spirit of the Lord came upon me and as I spoke the words, "In the name of Jesus . . . ," she fell backward under His power. She lay there, crumpled up like a rag doll, her wig off to one side and two black rivers of mascara streaming down her cheeks. When the meeting was over, she was still lying there on the floor, crying.

At Christmas I received a card. "Dear Wild Bill," it began, "if you are ever in Los Angeles, please drop by. I am a hostess in a restaurant and I'd like to see you again and tell you what has happened in my life."

Like a lot of other notes I receive, it got shuffled among the bills on my desk at home. Then one day I picked it up and took it to the office with me, never giving it much thought.

Forty-seven salesmen were working for me at that time, so there was always someone to go lunch with. But one lunch hour it so happened that my boss and all the salesmen were busy, even the custodian was busy. I would have been happy to take anybody to lunch, but the Lord had something else in mind.

The restaurant at which this lady worked was located in downtown Los Angeles, not far from my office, so I walked over to it. It looked like a nice place to eat, so I went in for lunch.

"How many, please?" the hostess asked.

"One," I answered.

We walked toward the bar and since I was alone I began to wonder if she was going to seat me there. ("Lord, not the bar, not the bar!") Having spent twenty-two years in bars, I'm not homesick for them. We passed into another room; it was rather cold, so the hostess seated me by the fireplace and handed me a menu.

After a while I became aware of someone's presence in the room. I glanced up from my menu, and there, leaning against the doorway, was the hostess, crying. I thought to myself, "Am I that offensive? Maybe she's crying because I'm by myself."

I turned to her and asked, "Is there anything wrong?"

"Wild Bill," she answered, "don't you recognize me?"

I was looking at a woman with close-cropped, reddish-brown hair, dressed in a turtleneck sweater and a long skirt.

"No, I don't recognize you," I confessed.

"My name is Patty."

Suddenly I realized that this was the lady whom we had left lying on the floor at the Capistrano Valley chapter meeting with the black mascara rivers flowing down her cheeks.

"You know, Wild Bill," she confided in me, "it's been two hundred days since I last had a drink. I was saved that night you prayed for me."

The waitress came in to take my order. "Have you decided what you want, sir?"

"I certainly have," I answered joyfully. "I'll have the largest steak you have in the house, the biggest baked potato, and *two hundred peas.*''

''Would you like to go over that again, please?'' she requested.

''I sure will. I'll have the largest steak in the house . . .''

''I got that.''

''. . . the biggest baked potato . . .''

''I got that too. Next part?''

''. . . and two hundred peas. Exactly. And if there's any problem with that, just ask Patty about it.''

I was rejoicing and praying in tongues when the waitress arrived with my meal. ''Here you are, sir. The largest steak we have in the house. The largest baked potato we have. And there are exactly two hundred peas—I counted them myself.''

Because I was so elated, I didn't eat too much of the steak, and I merely dabbled at the potato. But I ate every pea on the plate—and counted each one as I put it in my mouth! ''Thank You, Jesus . . . one. Thank You, Jesus . . . two. Thank You, Jesus . . . three.''

When I had counted all two hundred I said, ''Praise God, hallelujah, for the two-hundredth one!''

Patty's heart had been soft that night in Capistrano Valley, and God reached her. At another time in her life, she might have been as callous as that little old man in the airport at Dallas. Never waste an opportunity to tell someone about Jesus, even if they *are* drunk!

I was speaking one evening at a Full Gospel Business Men's rally in Ventura, California. When I left the platform it was necessary to walk around the outside of the room in order to get to the back row where Mavis was sitting. As I rounded a corner, there on the floor was a young waitress, sobbing her heart out.

"What's wrong?" I inquired.

"Look what happened," she sobbed, "chicken everywhere! And it's my first day on the job." She had knocked over a whole tray of chicken dinners; peas, potatoes and everything else had scattered everywhere.

"I can help you," I volunteered. I reached for a piece of chicken, grabbed a potato, and started to round up the peas. As I helped her clean up the mess, I asked, "Do you know Jesus Christ as your personal Savior?"

She stopped scraping up peas and stared at me for a moment. In my talk that evening I had told the story of Patty and the two hundred peas. "You're the fellow who just told about the peas, aren't you?" she asked.

"I'm the one," I answered.

"Gee," she said, "was that a true story?"

"You sound like my wife," I quipped. (Mavis had asked me the same question when she heard the story for the first time.)

"Yes," I assured her, "that was a true story."

"Honest?"

"Honest. Do you know Jesus?"

She thought for a moment, then confessed, "Well, I sure don't know Him like you know Him. I've been going to church for a long time and I'm fairly faithful; but the way you talk, I don't know Jesus."

"Would you like to know Him?" I pressed.

"Yes," she said, "I really would."

"Then why don't we invite Him into your life right here?" I ventured.

"Here?" She was a little embarrassed.

"Well, we're on our knees," I said. "What better time and place than right here and now?"

Every day God provides us with opportunities to reach out to people—opportunities that are not to be missed. He knew that I was going to walk around the corner at that precise instant, and that this was the best moment in this girl's life for her to hear the Gospel. Her heart was soft, she was ready to listen. Had I missed the opportunity, several years might have rolled by before she heard the message again, and by then circumstances might have caused her to have become hardened.

Today, perhaps on your job, in a restaurant, on a bus, or with someone who calls at your home, you will encounter a heart that is soft . . . a heart that is ready to hear the Good News. Will you neglect that opportunity? It may be the one time in that person's life in which he is ready to hear. Tomorrow he may be like the little old man in the Dallas airport, so hardened that he is beyond help.

You cannot avoid being either a savor of life, or a savor of death. If you touch those lives to whom the Holy Spirit leads you, you will have an opportunity to bring life to many of them. Tragically, there will always be some who do not respond.

"And who is adequate for such a task?" In and of ourselves, we are not adequate—none of us. But God has provided us with the power we need to be effective witnesses. He has not abandoned us to our own resources, or left us to our own devices, to try to persuade men in our own strength. He has equipped us through the Holy Spirit with gifts that are mighty to change human lives.

4

All in the Price of the Ticket

Words can be so empty. What people need is to see the power of God in action. It's when the layman knows the power at his command that things begin to happen.

A man in England had been saving for years to pay his voyage aboard one of the great ocean liners operating between London and New York. He had never been to the United States, and it had been his lifelong dream to one day come to this country. He had relatives in New York whom he had not seen in half a century. Now, at the age of seventy-five, he had finally scraped together enough money to make the trip. He booked the cheapest passage available, paid for his ticket, and went on board.

The man had brought packets of cheese and crackers on board with him, hopefully sufficient for every meal throughout the long Atlantic crossing, because he felt he could not afford to eat in the ship's dining room. As the liner sailed into New York harbor he decided to eat his last meal on deck so he could observe the beautiful skyline as they docked.

As the old man was finishing the last of his meager provisions, the purser came strolling along the deck. "Sir," he inquired, "why are you out here eating cheese and crackers? Dinner is being served in the dining room."

"Oh, you don't understand," replied the old man, "I have no money to eat dinner in the dining room; it took all the money I had to pay for passage on this ship."

"But, sir," the pursor responded, "didn't you know that the meals were included in the price of the ticket?"

Then, seeing the old man's stricken expression, he added, "Do you mean you've been eating cheese and crackers in your cabin the entire voyage? Why, sir, you could have been dining with the captain of the ship the whole time!"

A great many of our churches today are eating cheese and crackers, instead of dining with the Captain. They have their ticket to heaven—they have received salvation. But they are missing out on some of the greatest joys of being on board "that old Gospel ship." Jesus didn't come to this earth to die on the cross just so we believers could have eternal life; He also came that we might have *abundant* life. (John 10:10.) And His provision for that abundant life is the baptism in the Holy Spirit.

Speaking to the woman at the well in Samaria, "Jesus answered and said unto her, Whosoever drinketh of this water shall thirst again: but whosoever drinketh of the water that I shall give him shall never thirst; but the water that I shall give him shall be in him a well of water springing up into everlasting life" (John 4:13,14).

When we accept Jesus Christ as Savior and Lord, when we are born again, the Holy Spirit comes to reside within us so that we will never thirst. But Jesus went on to say, "He that believeth on me, as the scripture hath said, out of his belly shall flow rivers of living water" (John 7:38). Salvation is the wellspring, but the rivers of living water are the baptism in the Holy Spirit—being immersed in the river of the Spirit.

All believers have the Holy Spirit. "But ye are not

in the flesh, but in the Spirit, if so be that the Spirit of God dwell in you. Now if any man have not the Spirit of Christ, he is none of his'' (Rom. 8:9). But the Spirit which indwells us desires to immerse us in its flow so that we are caught up and borne on its rushing waters.

In chapters 40 through 48 of the book of Ezekiel a description is given of God's holy temple. This passage is not referring to the temple which was constructed on earth in the days of Solomon. Rather, it describes in ideal terms—in Old Covenant symbolism—the heavenly temple of God.

In John 4:20 the woman at the well said to Jesus, ''Our fathers worshipped in this mountain; and ye say, that in Jerusalem is the place where men ought to worship.'' How did Jesus answer her? He explained that under God's new agreement with man—the New Covenent—worship is no longer a matter of a physical temple and an earthly location. ''Jesus saith unto her, Woman, believe me, the hour cometh, when ye shall neither in this mountain, nor yet at Jerusalem, worship the Father . . .. But the hour cometh, and now is, when the true worshippers shall worship the Father in spirit and in truth: for the Father seeketh such to worship him. God is a Spirit: and they that worship him must worship him in spirit and in truth'' (John 4:21-24).

Today, God's temple is not physical, it is spiritual. *We* are that temple. ''Now therefore, ye are no more strangers and foreigners, but fellowcitizens with the saints, and of the household of God; and are built upon the foundation of the apostles and prophets, Jesus Christ himself being the chief corner stone; in whom all the building fitly framed together groweth unto an holy temple in the Lord: in whom ye also are builded together for an habitation of God through the Spirit" (Eph 2:19-22). What Ezekiel described in ideal Old-Covenant terminology is God's spiritual temple, the Church.

In Ezekiel 47 water is seen to flow from the altar. At first the water was only ankle-deep. When it was measured again, it was knee-deep. On the third measuring, ". . . it was a river that (Ezekiel) could not pass over: for the waters were risen, waters to swim in, a river that could not be passed over" (v. 5).

This is the river of living water of which Jesus spoke. As it flows into the sea, ". . . it shall come to pass, that every thing that liveth, which moveth, whithersoever the rivers shall come, shall live: and there shall be a very great multitude of fish, because these waters shall come thither: for they shall be healed; and every thing shall live whither the river cometh" (Ezek. 47:9). On the banks of the river grow trees for food," . . . whose leaf shall not fade, neither shall the fruit thereof be consumed: it shall bring forth new fruit according to his months, because their waters they issued out of the sanctuary: and the fruit thereof shall be for meat, and the leaf thereof for medicine" (Ezek.47:12).

Jesus was begotten by the Holy Spirit; He had the Spirit from birth. When the time came for Him to begin His ministry, the Spirit descended upon Him like a dove. (Luke 3:22.) He was now immersed in the Spirit—baptized in the Spirit—full of the Spirit. "And Jesus returned in the power of the Spirit unto Galilee," we are told in Luke 4:14. From that point on He began to preach and to heal. Consistently we read that He preached the Good News of the reign of God and healed all who were sick. Both in the ministry of Jesus and the ministry of the Early Church, healing accompanied the outpouring of rivers of living water—the baptism of the Holy Spirit.

We can wade in the Spirit, or we can paddle in the Spirit; in either case, we still have our feet on the ground. What God wants us to do is to let go and allow His Spirit to bear us up in its flow. A lot of believers are wading—they know the Lord, but that's as far as it goes. Others are paddling around—but they're not prepared to "launch out into the deep" and abandon themselves totally to the Spirit's control. But we shall only know the power of the Spirit and see it minister healing to the nations when we allow ourselves to be lifted off our feet and immersed in its flow.

The same power to minister life and healing is available to every believer. I know, because I've experienced it myself and I have seen others experience it. I've seen miracles happen because people believed in the power of the Holy Spirit. I would like to share some of those miracles with you.

In a church in Melbourne, Australia, I was seated on the platform behind the piano and the organ. As I sat listening to the pastor deliver the message, suddenly the Lord spoke to me. "Wild Bill, I want you to go to that girl sitting over there in the wheelchair."

"Fine, Lord," I answered. "When it's time for the altar call I'll sure do that."

I continued listening to the message. Again the Lord spoke: "Wild Bill, I want you to minister over there."

"Lord, I'm going to, just as soon as the message

is over. I can't get out right now—I'm jammed in here behind the piano and the organ.''

"I want you to go directly over there.''

"Lord,'' I protested, "the pastor is speaking in front of me. There are three or four steps down in front of the podium, and there are 900 people in this auditorium.''

I have learned through the years that it really doesn't do any good to try to argue with the Lord, so after a few minutes of procrastination I gave in. "All right, Lord,'' I said, "I'll do it.''

I waited for the pastor to pause to take a breath. No pause came. Finally the Lord simply ordered me. "Go now!'' I got up from my seat, walked right in front of the pastor and went over to the girl in the wheelchair. There was a pause then all right! Out of the corner of my eye I could see that people were looking at me. The pastor resumed speaking, but the congregation had one eye on me and one eye on him.

I said to the young lady, "The Lord has just instructed me to pray for you.'' She had had polio—one of her legs was paralyzed and withered from lack of use.

Immediately her mother chimed in: "Oh no, I don't want you to pray for her. Every evangelist who has ever come into this town with any type of healing ministry—everyone with a bottle of oil in his hand to anoint her with—has prayed for her. She's been disappointed so many times. I don't want you to pray for her.''

"I'm not talking to you, ma'am,'' I said courteously. "I'm talking to your daughter.''

The girl was about eighteen, so I asked her, "Do you want to be healed? Do you believe in it?''

"Yes, I believe in it," she answered.

"Then the Lord can heal you," I assured her.

Her mother grabbed hold of her so I turned to the mother and said, "Just a minute. You can cry in your handkerchief if you want to, but we are going to pray."

The withered leg looked just like a broomstick. The girl had a long metal brace on it and walked with canes that had straps around them. I asked her mother, "Would you mind taking the brace off?" So she did.

The girl was wearing a three-inch-high shoe on that foot, so I instructed her mother, "Take off her shoe also."

The message was winding to a close and people were beginning to crowd around us. Suddenly the girl's leg began to vibrate in my hand and I felt it move out. Then it began to jerk. During the next eighteen minutes I watched that leg grow out a full three inches! It was still as thin as a broomstick, but it was normal length.

"Would you stand up now?" I said. The girl stood up, without the help of her brace and without her shoe.

"Walk over to the podium and back," I instructed. By now the altar call was over and everyone was watching. She walked to the altar and back again, with a slight limp.

"You can do better than that," I urged. "The Lord has strengthened your leg. I want you to *walk* up there." She started walking almost normally.

We had to leave Melbourne for our next engagement in Adelaide, several hundred miles away. Our first night there was at Apollo Stadium. At the close of the service a great many people came forward for prayer. When I minister to people who are in the line for ministry, I don't notice faces too much; the Holy

Spirit reveals to me their need by the word of knowledge. As I proceeded along the line I stopped in front of two ladies. The Spirit said nothing to me about their need, so I looked at them and asked, "What do you want me to pray about?"

They were obviously mother and daughter. The daughter's eyes filled with tears. She said, "Wild Bill, don't you recognize me?"

I looked at her and said, "No, I don't think I do. Your mother's face is familiar, but I don't recognize you."

"Well, I'm Trudy," she said. "Two days ago you prayed for me in Melbourne."

"You're the girl in the wheelchair!" I exclaimed.

"Yes," she answered.

"Tell me the story," I said excitedly.

"That's why I'm down here," she began. "After you got through and were talking to those people the other night, I went home. I felt so good because my leg had grown out. I've been a victim of polio since I was two years of age. That night as I undressed in front of the mirror I looked at my little leg and I said, 'O God, if Wild Bill can believe, why can't I? I want to believe that when I get up in the morning my leg is going to be fully healed. Thank You, Lord.'

"Next morning I woke up and leaped out of bed with a scream. My momma rushed in crying, 'What's wrong?' I said, 'Look at me, Momma; look at me!' My leg had grown back to its normal size during the night!

"My momma said to me, 'What do you want to do?'

"'The first thing I want to do is go out and buy a street-length dress because I've never owned one,' I told her. 'The next thing I want to do is go show my pastor. Then I want to drive around and show all my friends what has happened to me. And, Momma, it's six hundred miles . . . but can we drive down to Adelaide to see Wild Bill?'''

Now I don't have a great healing ministry. I'm no healer; I can't heal anyone. I'm just a person who lets the living waters of the Holy Spirit catch me up off my feet and bear me wherever God wants me. The Lord wants to minister that way through all of us. "And these signs shall follow them that believe," Jesus promised, "In my name shall they cast out devils; they shall speak with new tongues; they shall take up serpents; and if they drink any deadly thing, it shall not hurt them; they shall lay hands on the sick, and they shall recover" (Mark 16:17,18). If you are a believer, God can do mighty things through you as you allow His Holy Spirit to fill you and flow through you.

The restoration of Trudy's leg was a *creative* miracle because God caused a leg to grow out to normal size. While in Australia I was present when another tremendous healing miracle took place.

The second night at Apollo Stadium, as we went out onto the platform, the preacher pointed up toward the second balcony.

"Would that young lady up there please stand up?" he said, and the young woman to whom he pointed rose to her feet.

"The Lord just spoke to me through a word of knowledge and told me that you have a lump in your left breast," explained the preacher. "God is healing you right now. I want you to go to the restroom and examine yourself, and then report to the usher whether what I have spoken is correct." She agreed to do so.

Pretty soon news came to the platform to confirm

the word which had been given the young lady. During the meeting the Lord worked a miracle of healing and the lump completely dissolved.

Later on, Harold Lawrence, an international director for the Full Gospel Business Men's Fellowship in Australia, told me that this young woman showed a pastor's wife where the nodule had disappeared from her breast. The pastor's wife observed that the young lady's right breast had been surgically removed when she had developed cancer five years earlier.

That evening God had healed a diseased body—but during the night, while the young lady slept, He performed a *creative* miracle as well! The next morning the pastor's wife received a call from the excited young lady who explained that during the night a new breast had grown out on her right side, a perfect match to the one on the left!

This is just one evidence of God's power to perform creative miracles for those who believe.

Why did the world sit up and take notice of Jesus when He was on earth? It wasn't just His message that grabbed their attention; it was His demonstration of the power of God through miracles. Words alone are not going to win the world to Christ. Paul testified to the church in Corinth which he had established: ''And when I came to you, brethren, I did not come with superiority of speech or of wisdom, proclaiming to you the testimony of God. For I determined to know nothing among you except Jesus Christ, and Him crucified. And I was with you in weakness and in fear and in much trembling. And my message and my preaching were not in persuasive words of wisdom, but in demonstration of the Spirit and of power, that your faith should not rest on the wisdom of men, but on the power of God'' (1 Cor. 2:1-5 NAS).

No one evangelist can reach the world. What God wants is for the laymen to arise, filled with the Holy Spirit, and go out to minister to people with a demonstration of the power of God. Only when ordinary men and women in regular jobs and from every walk of life utilize the gifts of the Holy Spirit to minister physical, mental, emotional, financial and spiritual healing to the nations are we going to evangelize the world.

I receive a lot of letters from people all over the globe, but some of them touch my heart in a special way. A girl by the name of Adrian Strata wrote me. She was about twenty-five years old, and had a large hump on her back. One of her legs dragged—it didn't function like a leg at all.

''Dear Bill,'' she wrote, ''I just wanted to tell you what the Lord has done for me since you left. My leg is healing and the hump on my back is getting much smaller. In fact, it is getting better every day. I have been shouting 'glory' to it . . . and God is healing it. Praise the Lord! Thank you for praying for me, and may God richly bless you.''

''Would you please come forward?'' I said to a lady in one of our meetings. She came to the platform and I said to her, ''The Lord told me that you have a short leg.'' One of her legs was about an inch and a half shorter than the other. As I talked with her I learned that she had a Ph.D. in music and was a professor at the university. We prayed for her and her leg lengthened.

About a month later we were in the same area and this lady came up to me excitedly.

"Do you remember when you called me out of the audience?" she asked.

"I sure do."

"Well, something wonderful happened to me."

"Yes, I know, your leg grew out."

"Yes, I had been having trouble with that leg for a long time. I had had four operations on it. You didn't see all the scars on it. But when I got home something wonderful happened. When I took my dress off I saw that all those ugly scars had disappeared!"

All around the world ordinary people like me, who have never had formal theological training, are learning that God has provided us with the gifts of the Holy Spirit so we can minister in power to those in need.

On another occasion in Australia, I was having dinner with a group of ministers in the Wentworth Hotel in Sydney. The conversation centered around the meaning of a particular Greek word. I became bored with the discussion and excused myself from the table. I walked out into the lobby and took a seat. Pretty soon an elderly couple came up to me. The man was hobbling along with the help of a cane.

"Wild Bill," he said, "I just heard your testimony. Is it really true that you were saved on the roof of a Baptist church?"

I assured him that the story was true.

"Well," he mused, "that's interesting. Our church building is so old that they wanted to tear it down, but of all people the Communist party campaigned to preserve it, because it is a historical landmark." (Can you imagine the Communists doing that?)

"My father was a deacon in that church, as was his father before him," continued the old man. "In fact, my family has had at least one representative in the leadership of that church for over a hundred years. I myself have been an elder in it for years and years. But I don't understand what you mean when you talk about knowing Jesus personally. I know Him in the Bible, but I don't really know Him as you do. You talk as if you have a relationship with Him, as though you talk with Him every day."

"Brother, I do," I said. "He's my best friend. I put Him before my family, my job, everything. He's Number One in my life."

"I don't have that feeling," he confessed.

"Well, you can," I told him. I began to tell him about my relationship with Jesus, eventually coming to my favorite Bible passage, Romans 10:9,10.

"That's beautiful," he said. "If I believe in my heart and confess with my mouth . . ."

". . . you will be saved," I confirmed.

"Well, I believe in my heart," he acknowledged. "Now how do I confess with my mouth?"

"Let's kneel right here," I urged.

"In the lobby of the hotel?"

"Best place I know of."

So the old man and his wife knelt with me by the elevator and I led them both through the sinner's prayer. When we rose to our feet I hugged them both.

"Am I saved?" he asked.

I said, "Brother, you are saved!" My spirit rejoiced as I watched them go on their way.

About that time the pastors came out of the restaurant, totally unaware of what had just taken place during their debate. They were still discussing the meaning of that seemingly all-important Greek word.

Later I picked up my Bible and read Proverbs 11:30: "The fruit of the righteous is a tree of life; and he that winneth souls is *wise*." Now I am not belittling the value of scholarship—it can be a great asset to the child of God. But I thank God that our effectiveness as witnesses is not dependent upon our knowledge of ancient Hebrew and Greek, that those of us with little human wisdom or knowledge can also win souls to the Lord because we have the power of God within us!

Jesus has sent us out to preach the Good News, "not in persuasive words of wisdom, but *in demonstration of the Spirit and of power*." That is how we need to minister to the masses, with the gifts of the Spirit, always tempered by the fruit of the Spirit.

While in Guatemala I saw thirty thousand people who were living in the space of eighty acres. They had come there during the earthquake which had struck their land two years earlier. They lived in hovels—little shacks with bare floors, wooden sides and tin roofs. There were no cooking facilities, no bathrooms. Many times a dozen or more people occupied a room measuring no more that twenty feet square.

A little girl there, who was about five and a half years old, stood only twenty-nine inches high and weighed a mere twenty-one and a half pounds. Many of the children had worms crawling out of their mouths and ears, and lice in their hair.

We visited a missionary who feeds about forty children a day on tortillas and beans and other such bland foods; he can't feed them anything more nourishing because their systems can't take it. They come in to eat, sing a few songs, and hear about Jesus. Mentally, they understand; but not in their hearts, because when they go home their folks tell them, ''Don't believe what those foreigners tell you!''

No amount of argument will convince people in such an environment; they must see the power of God demonstrated.

There was a little boy there whose eyes were covered with a white film. The Spirit drew me over to him. Placing my hands over his eyes, I began to pray for him. When I removed my hands from his eyes, two white patches remained in my hands. In an instant his sight returned!

When people live in the midst of a cesspool and survive from one meager meal to the next, without any hope in life, their primary need isn't to know the meaning of Greek words—as good as that may be. They need to experience the power of the Holy Spirit to deliver and heal them of their afflictions.

Jesus has commissioned us to go out into the highways and byways of life, to compel the poor, the blind, the lame and the beggars to come into His Kingdom— and such people are not concerned about Greek. Neither am I — I have enough difficulty handling English properly.

You and I may not be versed in the intricacies of ancient Hebrew and Greek. We may not be able to analyze the Scriptures in their original languages or to expound on them in a scholarly fashion. But we *can* minister in love and in the power of the Holy Spirit. That privilege is included in the price of the ticket. If you're still subsisting on cheese and crackers, take your rightful place in the dining room with the Captain. He has provided a rich feast for you to enjoy and to share with others.

5
Too Much to Ask

It's dark behind the Iron Curtain, but a small band of believers there are carrying a torch for Jesus. My visit to Yugoslavia jolted me out of my complacency. I found out what it really means to be a Christian!

"Wild Bill, what are you going to leave here in Yugoslavia?"

It was the morning of our departure. The local pastor was to drive us into Belgrade to catch our plane back to the United States. He had arrived right on time and I was waiting on the curb in front of the hotel after descending the four flights of stairs carrying my bags. Opening the trunk of the car, the pastor helped me load my things, then ran back upstairs to assist my friend with his belongings.

I had chosen the back seat for this leg of the journey. My traveling companion was very tall so I wanted him to enjoy the front seat. Besides, I thought that *his* knuckles ought to be white for a change. In the back seat I could shut my eyes and no one would see my reaction to the pastor's engaging in the Yugoslavian version of "chicken."

I looked at Jelena who sat beside me. Her hair was pulled up in a bun, she wore no make-up, and her clothes were worn and tattered. She looked to be around sixty-five, even though I knew that in reality she was only about my age. As I watched her, the Lord spoke to me. "Wild Bill, what are you going to leave here in Yugoslavia?"

I was puzzled. "Lord, You know what I have

already done," I responded defensively. "I gave the pastor a shortwave cassette radio so he can listen to the Far Eastern Broadcasting Company and the Voice of America."

The voice came again. "Wild Bill, what are you going to leave in Yugoslavia?"

"Well, I also gave to the church and school that we visited in Zagreb. And I've made donations to a number of individuals in various places. Most of my giving was done in secret; in fact, my left hand didn't know what my right hand was doing."

As I reflected on the people I had helped, I felt pretty good. Yes, I had definitely done my share—and more. The pastor would soon be down with the rest of our bags and I could go on my way secure in the knowledge that I had more than fulfilled my duty toward these people. As the moment of our departure approached, the Lord spoke again. "Wild Bill, what are you going to leave in Yugoslavia?"

What was the Lord getting at? I had ministered to people and given money to the needy. What more could I do? Yet he seemed to want more from me, something of a personal nature. "What are You trying to tell me, Lord?"

Suddenly I felt my Bible burn in my hand. "No, Lord," I resisted, "that's the one thing I am not going to give up! You are *not* going to take this Bible from me."

Before I was saved I had never read a Bible in my life. The day I came to know the Lord I bought a big Bible with large, clear print. I was so proud of it. It had a distinctive black cover and many of the most famous stories within its pages were illustrated by beautiful color plates. It had become my most prized possession in the days subsequent to my conversion because I had carefully underlined in it passages which were landmarks in my Christian walk.

As I sat in the back seat of the car and fought with the Lord's request, it was as if my life flashed before my eyes. I remembered the day that I gave the Lord my heart on the roof of the Baptist church, and the passage I had underlined in my new Bible that day—Romans 10:9,10. It had become my favorite of all Scriptures and I had turned to it countless times to lead others to the Lord.

I thought back to that glorious day when I was delivered from drunkenness. I had underlined Joel 2:32 on that occasion: "And it shall come to pass, that whosoever shall call on the name of the Lord shall be delivered." God had so faithfully fulfilled His promise, freeing me from my slavery to the bottle. I had not touched a drop of alcohol in the several years that had gone by since that day.

In the years that I was a drunk, one of my sons had run away from home and sought refuge in a life of drugs. After my conversion, the Lord had led me to Jeremiah 31:16 where He promised us concerning our children: "Refrain thy voice from weeping, and thine eyes from tears: for thy work shall be rewarded, saith the Lord; and they shall come again from the land of the enemy." Not only had I underlined those words, I had written beside them, "Claimed June 15,1974." When God fulfilled His promise to me, I had turned to the passage once more and written, "Answered October 10, 1974."

My thoughts wandered to 1 Samuel 10:1-9 where Samuel poured a flask of oil on the head of Saul to anoint him king, and the oil had run down over all his vestments. In verse nine I had underlined the words "God gave him another heart." God changed my heart too on the day He baptized me in the Holy Spirit, symbolized by the oil with which Samuel anointed Saul. That change came about in this way:

Louie, our youngest son, was the first to receive the baptism of the Holy Spirit; he was only fourteen years old at the time. Shortly after, Mavis also received the baptism. They began leaving little hints around the house—tracts and books on receiving the baptism. I noticed a change in them both, but I was still fighting against it. "Don't rush me, don't rush me, I don't want to hear anything about that!" I would tell them, sometimes a little angered by their persistence.

We were having a prayer meeting for young people at our home and many of them were receiving the baptism. I was a little irritated that day because all the attention wasn't on me. "Well, you can join us," Mavis invited, but I didn't want to do that. Instead I lay on my bed listening to a John Hall record.

There was a particularly anointed song on the record which talked about rivers of living water flowing out from us. As I lay on my bed, completely relaxed, those rivers suddenly began to gush forth from my innermost being! I wasn't asking, I wasn't *seeking* —it just overtook me! A tongue began to pour forth out of my mouth and I couldn't stop it. I went down to the living room to find Mavis and beckoned her to follow me. We went down the hall and I kept pointing to my mouth. "I can't stop" was all I was able to tell her.

Mavis knew instantly what had happened. "That's fine, dear, " she reassured me, "just go back and enjoy it." I had heard of people receiving the baptism of the Spirit in some odd ways, such as while driving down the freeway or taking a shower, but mine was the strangest of all. I wasn't trying a bit, it just came over me.

Then there had come that day when the Lord said to me, ''Wild Bill, I am calling you into the ministry.'' I could picture the words I had underlined in my Bible that day.

''Oh, no You're not, Lord,'' I had argued. ''I've tried to serve You well. I've rebuilt my life and now I'm making a lot of money. I'm vice-president of a title company. My territory covers five counties. I'm a big shot here. You can't do this to me!''

''Read Isaiah 6:8,'' He continued. I turned to the passage and read it: ''Also I heard the voice of the Lord, saying, Whom shall I send, and who will go for us? Then said I, Here am I; send me.''

''That's you, Wild Bill,'' the Lord said. ''I'm sending *you*.''

I remembered those agonizing moments in the hospital room following my operation for a torn retina, when Satan whispered to me that my healing ministry was over. What comfort I had received from the passage the Lord had brought before my mind on that occasion! ''For God hath not given us the spirit of fear; but of power, and of love, and of a sound mind'' (2 Tim. 1:7). My eyes were bandaged, so I would ask the nurses who came into my room, ''Read the underlined part on page 1378 for me.''

I felt so comfortable with this Bible; I knew where to find all the passages that had such great meaning to me. And now the Lord was asking me to leave it behind in Yugoslavia!

''No, Lord, I can't do that. But I'll tell You what

I'll do; when I get back home I'll buy a brand new Bible. My old one cost only $14 and now they are $21. And I'll pay the postage to send it here."

Again the Lord spoke, "Wild Bill, what are you going to leave in Yugoslavia?"

"Well, Lord, I guess You want me to leave my Bible." We were nearly ready to leave. "I sure love that Bible," I rambled on, stalling for time. "It sure feels good in my hand, Lord. I would feel naked without it."

"Wild Bill," the Lord persisted, "what are you going to leave in Yugoslavia?"

I looked at Jelena. She had first noticed my Bible while I was enjoying a meal in her home. We had eaten lunch at her house every day, but I noticed that she never ate with us. There is a custom in many countries that the women eat after the men, so I didn't think too much about it. I assumed this was the custom in Yugoslavia. It was only later that I found out why she didn't sit down to eat with us: there was not enough food to go around. I had no idea her family was so poor. When I looked in her closet I discovered that she had only two changes of clothes!

On this particular day I had left the table during the meal and found Jelena looking at my Bible. As I approached her, she moved away. I said, "Jelena, would you like me to share some special memories with you?"

"Oh, yes!" she responded with excitement.

"See, here is a photograph of the Garden of Gethsemane," I began to explain. "It's taken from a position where you can look right through all those beautiful olive trees and see the Eastern Gate. One day when Jesus returns to this earth He is going to come down from the Mount of Olives, walk down the victory trail, cross through the Garden of Gethsemane, over the Kidron valley, and enter the city of Jerusalem through that very gate." Her eyes lit up as she looked at the picture.

"And here's a picture of the Jordan River," I continued. "That's where I baptized our youngest son, Louie." This was tremendously exciting to her.

"Ah, this is a picture of the tomb in which Lazarus was buried. Actually, there were two miracles at that tomb. The first was his resurrection from the dead. The second was his walking up the thirty-five steps that lead out of the tomb, still bound in his burial clothes."

"Can you read English, Jelena?"

"Yah, yah," she answered. "I like to touch your Bible, look at the pretty pictures, and read about Jesus." After that, I noticed her going through my Bible on several occasions.

My baggage was all loaded; there wasn't much time left. As I thought about how much my Bible meant to Jelena, the Lord asked me one more time, "Wild Bill, what are you going to leave in Yugoslavia?"

"Jelena," I began. She turned to look at me. "I've got something for you. I would like for you to have my Bible." I have seen many expressions of gratitude from people to whom I have given gifts, but never have I seen as much as I witnessed on Jelena's face that day as I handed her my precious Bible. As she clutched it to her breast, tears welled up in her eyes and she began to sob.

My time in Yugoslavia had been unlike any

experience of my life. Before I had left California, Mavis had given me a Scripture verse for my journey. ''For he shall give his angels charge over thee,'' she had read from Psalm 91:11, ''to guard thee in all thy ways.'' I had held on to that Scripture from the moment our giant 747 jet touched down in Belgrade until our final departure. It was my source of comfort and assurance, not only on the perilous roads where it seemed that ox carts, bicycles, buses, trucks and cars all claimed equal right of way, but in every situation we encountered during our fourteen-day visit to this Communist nation where no one seemed to speak English but us.

Our stay had begun in a castle which had been converted into a beautiful hotel. The Yugoslavs had built it in the 16th century to keep out the Turks. As we entered our room the local pastor whispered, ''Your room is bugged.''

''You're kidding,'' I said. I thought he had seen too many spy movies.

''No, I'm not,'' he assured me quietly. ''Watch!'' He climbed up on a chair and reached up to the screen that covered the air conditioning vent. He silently turned the screws that held the screen in place, then removed it to reveal the microphone that was suspended inside.

Each night I stood under the vent and preached. ''Pastor,'' I would say, ''did you know that in Romans 10:9,10 the Bible says that Jesus died for us and that if a person confesses with his mouth and believes with his heart, he can be saved?''

''No, I didn't know that, Wild Bill. Tell me, what does it say in the Twenty-third Psalm? That's somewhere in the Bible too, isn't it?''

We started out sharing a room together, but it

wasn't long before we found ourselves assigned to separate rooms! Not having anyone to share the Gospel with anymore, I used to spend my evenings reading the Bible aloud. I began in Genesis and read all the way through to Revelation. I was determined that the person listening on the other end of the bug was going to hear the Good News whether he wanted to or not!

There were no screens on the windows, so sometimes in the evenings I sat on my windowsill looking out over the Danube River and the city on the other side of its banks. There is nothing beautiful about the fabled ''beautiful blue Danube.'' Its waters, plowed endlessly by Russian trawlers, are murky and oily. As I contemplated the twenty-one million people who lived in this land, I was profoundly moved by the realization that fewer than ten thousand of them are born-again Christians.

I fell in love with the Yugoslavian brethren. They couldn't understand me and I couldn't understand them, but as I spoke to them through an interpreter the love flowed back and forth between our hearts. I was privileged to speak in a lot of small churches.

The people came to those meetings bundled up in huge coats. Their buildings were ice cold because they couldn't afford to heat them. Instead the people who came wore several layers of garments. The usual dress was a heavy topcoat, a jacket, a vest and a sweater. But despite their poverty, these wonderful people had extremely warm hearts.

During part of the trip I stayed with the parents of Erika, a Yugoslavian girl who resides in the United States and who is married to one of my best friends, Otis Wilson. Erika's folks called their home an apartment;

I would call it a room. We walked up three flights of stairs to reach it. There was no heat in the building at all. The bathroom was a considerable distance down the corridor; to take a shower it was necessary to go up another flight of stairs to the next floor.

This couple had gone through an extremely difficult time during World War II. Because the husband had refused to deny Jesus Christ, he was placed in a concentration camp. For four or five years his family had absolutely no visible means of support. At dinner time they had simply sat down at an empty table and thanked God for their dinner. Many times a knock would come at the door and someone would leave an egg or green vegetables.

In Yugoslavia if a person chooses to become a Christian, he gives up all rights to enter professional life. There is no possibility of his ever becoming a doctor or engineer. He is considered an outcast; in the eyes of the state he is nothing. That means he walks back and forth into town to work. And it's cold and snowing much of the year. It's a hard life.

I watched as women worked in the fields. I thought they were sixty years of age, but I learned that they were around thirty. Their hands were callused, their faces wrinkled, their eyes drawn, their bodies terribly thin. They were using sickles like the men, cutting down the corn that was ready to harvest. The only job they didn't do alongside the men was to lather down the horses at the end of the workday; instead, they returned home to cook the evening meal.

I was terribly saddened by the elderly because they had no hope in life. They were no longer productive because they didn't have the strength to push the wheelbarrows anymore, so they sat along the roadsides, gazing at the houses from which the paint was peeling. They were just waiting to die. I saw lots of little old ladies who had nothing in life to interest them except to sweep the streets.

If a member of a Yugoslavian family dies—whether it's the father or mother, son or daughter—custom demands that the family mourners wear black for the rest of their lives. So many people are dressed in black there that it seems the only ones not wearing it are those in military uniforms: one-quarter of the people you meet as you walk down the streets of the cities carry sidearms.

I think it was the young people who touched my heart the most. I cried every night as I looked across the street and saw boys and girls, seventeen or eighteen years of age, with nothing to do but stand around on street corners and smoke cigarettes—their one form of entertainment. There are no bowling alleys, no ice skating rinks, no movies. I wanted so desperately to tell them the Gospel of Jesus Christ. But I was handicapped. Although they were just standing or walking aimlessly, I was forbidden to go up to them and talk to them about Jesus. Had I done so, I probably would not be here now writing this book.

One of the greatest privileges I had was to baptize several people in one of the underground churches. Since there was no baptistry, we cut a hole in the ground, three feet by six, not quite deep enough to cover the person. All day long the women of the church brought glasses and tea kettles of water hidden in their aprons, enough to finally fill the hole. A baptism couldn't take place at a regular service because the meetings were bugged and secret service police kept an eye on them, so we came together secretly at night. It made me think back to the comfort of the United States where we baptize people in elaborate baptistries in magnificent churches with their stained-glass windows, lush carpets and padded pews. It requires great courage and self-sacrifice to become a baptized member of the Church in Yugoslavia.

At one meeting I was baptizing a rather large lady. The water was only three inches deep, so I flipped her over on both sides. It was the only way to immerse her! I had her half-way turned when a man announced, "The Holy Spirit has just told me that the police are coming." Everyone left in a hurry. I just had to drop the lady, and we both ran for cover.

In the underground churches the meetings begin when the first two people arrive. There are no announcements on television or radio—no bulletins or advertisements in the newspapers. The pastor simply tells one of the people, "We will have a church service on Sunday at 4:00 p.m." The rest of the people learn about the service by word of mouth.

At one of our meetings a brother said, "Wild Bill, the Holy Spirit just told me that there are going to be sixty people here tonight." After a period of time fifty-nine people were gathered together, and when I walked in we numbered sixty. The Yugoslavian churches rely totally on the Holy Spirit for the functioning of their services. That night the Holy Spirit moved mightily. No sooner had we vacated the building than a Mercedes pulled up and the police arrived.

One night I noticed that the brethren were all huddled around a small car. The doors were open and the hood was up. I walked over to them and asked, "What's the problem?"

"We stopped the car to pick up some people and

it went dead,'' they explained.

Everyone was scurrying around like beavers, trying to get it to start. ''Just a minute,'' I interjected, ''have you prayed?''

''No,'' they confessed.

''Well, I'll show you how to do it,'' I said, stepping up to the car. ''In the name of Jesus!'' I shouted. Instantly the lights went on, the horn began sounding, and the engine started up.

''He's got the power!'' everyone exclaimed. All the police forces of Yugoslavia could not have touched me at that moment, I was so full of Jesus.

On one occasion I was praying for a lady in the pastor's church. As I laid my hands on her and asked that she receive the Holy Spirit, she began to say, ''Praise Jesus . . . praise Jesus!'' Thinking nothing of it, I passed on to the next person.

''Wild Bill,'' the interpreter said to me, ''this lady just received the heavenly language. She said, 'Praise Jesus!'''

''No, that's English,'' I said.

''Yes, but she's a Yugoslav,'' he explained ''and she can't speak English!''

It had been an eventful fourteen days, and the Lord had watched over us throughout our visit in accordance with His promise in Psalm 91:11. As we said our goodbyes and sped into Belgrade, I thought of the words of a popular song of the sixties: ''Who are all these lonely people, and where do they all come from?''

As the wheels of our 747 lifted off the ground, the Holy Spirit said to me, ''What's more important, Wild

Bill, is what is their final destination?''

My visit to Yugoslavia had jolted me out of the complacency that is so widespread in Western Christianity. Here were people who were risking their lives for Jesus, many of them in abject poverty. They flowed in the power of the Spirit, rejoicing in the Lord despite all their discomforts and persecution.

I felt ashamed as I thought of how reluctant I had been to leave my most precious possession behind, when Bibles are so scarce in Yugoslavia and so plentiful in America. How limited was my spirit of self-sacrifice compared with theirs! I had never seen so much zeal for God.

I can't change the situation in Yugoslavia; only God can draw back the Iron Curtain that enfolds those people in darkness. All I can do is pray for that day to come speedily.

But I can do something about the situation in which I find myself here in the West. What freedom we enjoy to witness for Jesus! Only when those opportunities are missing do we truly appreciate them. I came home resolved to use every opportunity that God affords me to spread the Good News.

The people of Yugoslavia are crying out for opportunities to share salvation with their nation, opportunities that we have in abundance. Is it too much to ask of us to share Jesus with people each day of our lives?

6

A Walrus Whisker
and a Seal's Tooth

They were all that he had . . . a walrus whisker and a seal's tooth. But he wanted me to have them as a token of his eternal gratitude for leading him to Jesus.

The mass of people thronging the Pan Am ticket desk were screaming and hollering obscenities. Some of them were waving their tickets in the air as they beseiged the lone, harried girl behind the counter.

"What's going on here?" I wondered as I strolled over to the counter.

Our Western Airlines flight had just landed in Seattle where I was planning to take a rest in the Pan Am Clipper Club before proceeding aboard a Pan Am flight to Alaska. The Pan Am desk was a scene of mass confusion, but I made my way through the crowd to the girl on duty, knocked on the counter and said, "Pardon me, miss; can you tell me where the Clipper Club is?"

"It's not open," she retorted.

"Oh," I said with an expression of surprise. "Is there a reason?"

"Yes, because your flight's canceled," she snapped.

"My flight's canceled?" I responded, even more surprised. "Why's that?"

"Because we're on strike, that's why. Everyone's on strike but me."

"Well, praise God," I said calmly. "May I ask you

a question? Do you think there is a possibility I could get a seat aboard another flight? Otherwise I'll have to go into Seattle and get a hotel room.''

She shook her head.

''Well, I know that God works everything out,'' I said. ''Romans 8:28 tells us that all things work together for good to those who love God and who are the called according to His purpose. Praise God, I guess He wants me to stay in Seattle tonight. Thank you very much.''

As I was retreating from the counter the girl shouted after me, ''Sir! Sir! Just a minute.''

I turned. ''Are you speaking to me?''

All the people who had been spewing out obscenities were suddenly quiet, their eyes focused on me. I walked back to the counter.

''Yes, ma'am?''

''What's wrong with you?'' she asked with a quizzical expression on her face.

''Nothing's wrong with me,'' I answered. ''I just passed a very pleasant four and a half hours on a plane, the service was wonderful, the food was good, and I feel great. Now I'm going into Seattle to find a hotel room.''

''But you are supposed to go to Fairbanks, aren't you?''

''Yes, but it's not my fault that I can't. If God wants me in Seattle, it is probably because there is someone I can minister to there.''

She looked down at the counter and said, ''Let me have your ticket.'' The people surrounding me had been waiting for hours, so they stared at me as I went ahead of them all. The airline agent grabbed my ticket, ran her finger down the flight list and said, ''Hmm.

There's one seat to Anchorage, first class; it leaves in fifteen minutes. You're on it."

"Oh," I said, still more surprised, "but I'm going to Fairbanks."

"I know you're going to Fairbanks," she explained, "but the next morning I can have you ticketed to Fairbanks from Anchorage on Air Alaska. Pan Am will fly you first class, then pay for your hotel room and all your food until you get to Fairbanks. Thank you very much."

I had only fifteen minutes to catch the plane. I crossed over to the luggage carrousel, confident that my bag would come off the Western Airlines flight in time. Sure enough, the first bag out was mine. I picked it up and asked the attendant, "Where is concourse 3-A?"

"It's a long way down there," he replied.

"I have eight minutes."

"You'll never make it," he assured me. "It'll take you ten minutes to get there."

"The plane will hold because Wild Bill is on his way," I shouted back over my shoulder, leaving him shaking his head in disbelief.

When I arrived at concourse 3-A the plane was already revving up its engines. No sooner had I clambered aboard than the flight crew shut the door. My coat almost got caught in the jetway. The stewardess ushered me to my first-class seat. A girl was assigned to the window seat next to me. Some girls look hard, and some look soft. This one was hard.

I had never sat in first class before. It was a pleasant surprise. In the usual aircraft seat I feel cramped and unable to move; this seat was actually wider than I am. The first thing the flight attendant asked me was, "What are you going to have to drink?"

"A Holy Spirit cocktail," I answered cheerfully and with a smile.

"I beg your pardon?"

"A Holy Spirit cocktail."

"What is that?"

"Just give me a glass of water and some ice cubes, that's enough. That's what I call a Holy Spirit cocktail."

"You're weird," the stewardess replied.

"I'm not weird," I countered. "The plane waited for me, didn't it?"

"Yes, we had to wait for you till you came."

"Then I'm not weird, I'm special!"

I turned to the girl who was sitting next to me and asked her, "Do you know that Jesus loves you?"

She practically climbed up the wall. "What did you say?"

I repeated my question. "Do you know that Jesus loves you?"

"What are you, a Jesus freak?"

"I don't know about the freak part, but I do love Jesus."

"Well," she said, "the answer to your question is no." It was obvious that she didn't want to talk, so I waited until I had my Holy Spirit cocktail.

"Are you saved?" I suddenly asked.

"What do you mean, 'Am I saved?'"

"Do you know Jesus Christ as your personal Savior?" I asked, making my question a little clearer.

"No, I don't know anybody as my personal Savior." She was sounding a little nettled.

I persisted, "Would you like to know Him?"

"I don't think I have the time," she sighed.

"I have the time," I rebounded, "and not only

do I have the time but I have an opportunity. You've got three and a half hours ahead of you to have to listen to me!''

"Well, if you are some kind of nut, go ahead and tell me about Him," she said in resignation, "but I won't listen." She picked up a magazine, about to bury herself in its pages.

"Just a minute!" I interrupted. I took out a copy of *Voice* magazine, a monthly witnessing tool published by the Full Gospel Business Men's Fellowship International. This particular issue had my testimony in it. I pushed it in front of her. "If you want to read a magazine," I said, "read this."

"I don't want it."

"Read it."

"All right, I'll read it." So she settled down to read the article. After a while she asked me, "Did this really happen to you?"

"You betcha. For twenty-two years I was a drunk. I had you fooled, didn't I? You had no idea that I used to be that kind of a person. Do you know what you look like to me? You look like a hooker." I knew that the Holy Spirit was talking through me.

"I am," she said with a shocked tone. "Does it show that much?"

"Yes, sister, it does; it shows that much."

"I was married and I have two children, but I left my husband," she began to explain. "You mentioned to me about knowing Jesus. Well, I used to go to church, a long time ago. I thought I knew God, but church is a bunch of garbage."

I felt deep compassion for this girl. "You know, you have fallen into a life of vile sin," I said, "but the Bible says in 1 John 1:9, 'If we confess our sins, he is faithful and just to forgive us our sins, and to cleanse us from all unrighteousness.' It also says over in Jeremiah 3:22 that the backslidden child should return, and that's you."

"You know those Scriptures pretty good, don't you?" she said.

"That's my job," I said. "Jesus sent me to you. There's another Scripture I want to share with you—Isaiah 1:18: 'Come now, and let us reason together, saith the Lord: though your sins be as scarlet, they shall be as white as snow; though they be red like crimson, they shall be as wool.' God also says in Revelation 3:4 that there are some who 'have not defiled their garments; and they shall walk with me in white: for they are worthy.'"

"I've done too many bad things," she said sadly.

"You haven't done half the bad things I have," I encouraged her, "because I was twice as old as you when I got saved."

"Yeah, but the Lord wouldn't forgive me."

"He will forgive you. He's only waiting for you to confess. Let's go back to where I started when I first got on this plane. Jesus loves you. He loves you so much that He gave His life for you. He paid the price of your sins so that you can be forgiven of those sins and spend eternity in heaven with Him. And all you have to do to receive that forgiveness is to confess with your mouth and believe in your heart." Then I read her Romans 10:9,10.

"You're kidding," she said. "That's too simple."

"That's exactly what I said on the roof of that Baptist church," I assured her. "But it's not too simple; it's the promise of God. Wouldn't you like to confess and believe?"

"Yes," she said, "I would like to."

"Then let's do it right now." We went through the sinner's prayer. At about thirty-five thousand feet of altitude, a little sister who was once full of sin became a child of God. Instead of being a drunkard, a drug addict and a hooker, she became a princess, a queen, a joint-heir with Jesus, and all her sins were forgiven and forgotten.

When the plane landed I went into Anchorage and stayed at the best hotel at Pan Am's expense. Why not? I'm a child of the King! I called the brothers that evening and told them I couldn't be at their breakfast meeting. Next morning, they called me back. "Wild Bill, there's a Full Gospel meeting in Anchorage today. It's in the same hotel you're staying in. Go down and meet with them."

I went to the meeting and had an opportunity to speak. I had to leave a little early so I wouldn't miss my plane. As I was leaving, one of the brothers called to me, "Hey, I am the director of the convention up here in November. Would you be one of our speakers? We'll fly you and your wife up."

"Praise God, you've got yourself a speaker!" I responded.

Another brother tapped me on the shoulder. "You remember me?" he asked. "I was in Sandpoint, Idaho, and you came there and ministered to me. You said that not only would I be saved, but that I would move from Sandpoint to start a new life and God would bless me. I was saved that night. I moved to Anchorage, and now I have one of the largest construction companies up here. My life has changed. Brother, I want you to be at that convention too."

It is a great privilege to travel around the world

and see how God will use me to touch others. A providential meeting here, a word there. It is all part of the Master Design. When we are open to be used by the Holy Spirit, we never run out of opportunities to be about the Lord's business. We usually have no idea of the impact that a moment of ministry in the right place can have. On a plane, in an airport, at a hotel; the people whom God brings across our paths are there for us to minister to. All it takes for us to be used is an inner ear that is tuned to the voice of the Spirit and the courage to act on the promptings He gives us.

That day I got to see beautiful Mount McKinley and all of the magnificent scenery surrounding it. Had I flown the night before as I had been scheduled to do, I would have missed this breathtaking part of God's world.

At the meeting that evening I told the story about how the Lord had asked me to give my Bible away in Yugoslavia. Since returning I had bought another Bible, this time priced at $21. I had spent considerable time marking it up, putting in most of the underlining and comments which had been in the original one.

By this time I was becoming accustomed to giving my Bible away. After replacing the Bible I left in Yugoslavia, I was in my office one day when my wife walked in.

"Honey," she began. I thought to myself, "Uh oh, I'm in trouble. What could I have done?" (When my wife calls me "honey," I know it's for a reason.)

"Yes, what is it, dear?" I responded rather suspiciously.

"I've got Karen Garland here," she announced.

"Well, bring her in."

"Guess what."

"What?"

"Karen has dyslexia."

"Oh, really? I hope it's not contagious."

"No, you don't understand. That means that she has vision problems. She reads back to front and the lines blur together. It's so frustrating for her to try to read she just gives up. She was baptized in the Holy Spirit at a women's Bible study, and the first thing she would like to do is to read the Bible. I know you have a nice Bible with large print . . ."

"Again, Lord?"

"Yes."

"Karen, here's a Bible I would like for you to have. It's already underlined—I've worked hard at marking it up—but go ahead and read it."

Shortly after that, I left on a trip to Australia. While I was gone, I received a beautiful note from Karen. In it she explained to me that she was twenty-seven years old, married, and had two children, but that all through school she had had to fake her way because of her dyslexia.

"This is a prayer God gave me for you the Sunday you left for Australia," the note read. "I wrote it in the front of the Bible you gave me. I wanted to be able to reread it every time I thought of you while you were gone. It blesses me to be allowed to know you through God's eyes even a little:

"'To God I pray, may Bill be called a mighty man of God. May wisdom be in his right hand and discernment in his left. Anoint his words that many would hear Jesus calling them through him. In Jesus' name

I pray, amen.'

"God loves you, Bill. May you always be called a servant of the Most High God."

I got a special deal on my next Bible. They were marked down to $10. This was the Bible I took with me to Fairbanks. I had marked it up once again, underlining all the verses that were meaningful to me.

After the meeting in Fairbanks a little old lady came up to me with a brand new Bible in her hand. It had a white cover and was still wrapped in cellophane. "That was really a nice story," she said. "I've bought Bibles for people too. I think you will probably give your Bible to somebody while you are up here and I have a brand new one for you. Would you like to have it?"

"Lay it on me, ma'am!" I said with gratitude.

I was staying at the Polaris Hotel, the largest in Fairbanks, owned by one of the members of the local Full Gospel Business Men's Fellowship. I was in a room on the eighth floor.

That night as I looked out my window, I could see the flashing neon sign of a bar about a block away. It was midnight, but at that northern latitude there was still a faint glow of light in the sky and I could see men lying in the doorways, sleeping under parked cars, or sprawled in the gutter. Others were staggering around the streets in a drunken stupor. Some were racing cars up and down, creating havoc.

To my left was another bar next to a vacant lot. The lot was littered with human beings who had bedded down there for the night. According to the weather forecast it was supposed to drop down to about twenty-eight degrees that night, so these poor wretches had covered themselves with newspapers for protection against the cold.

As I surveyed the tragic scene before my eyes, the words of Isaiah 59:6 weighed heavily upon me: ''Their webs shall not become garments, neither shall they cover themselves with their works: their works are works of iniquity, and the act of violence is in their hands.''

''Go down and minister to them.''

I knew that voice, but I couldn't believe what it was telling me.

''Lord, they'll kill me!''

''I want you to go down there. You will not be harmed. My Word says in 1 John 5:18 that 'he that is begotten of God keepeth himself, and that wicked one toucheth him not.'''

I changed my clothes, went down into the street, and wandered over to the bar. A great big Eskimo man was seated on one of the bar stools. I went up to the bar and sat down beside him.

The bartender asked, ''What do you want?''

''I'll have a Holy Spirit cocktail.'' People stopped their drinking and looked at me. The bartender just stared.

''I'm Big Ed the Moose,'' announced the Eskimo on the bar stool, turning to me. ''I run this town. I deal the dope, I sell the girls, I run everything.''

''Then might I have a Holy Spirit cocktail, please?''

''Give him what he wants,'' Big Ed ordered the bartender.

''How do you mix it?''

''Just give me a glass of water with some ice cubes in it.''

The bar reeked of dope; the air was heavy with the presence of the demons of hell. I watched as a group of men played pool, their hardened faces declaring their misery. The words of Isaiah 57:20,21 burned within me: ''But the wicked are like the troubled sea, when it cannot rest, whose waters cast up mire and dirt. There is no peace, saith my God, to the wicked.''

I began to preach. Nobody was listening to me. They carried on with their drinking, their raucous laughter, their game of pool. I was having a hard time making myself heard above the din.

''QUIET!''

Pool cues froze, beer mugs stopped in mid-air, and silence descended upon the entire bar. You could have heard a pin drop. Even the ball stopped in the middle of the pool table!

''The preacher boy wants to say something,'' thundered Big Ed. Man, did I ever have respect then!

I preached my heart out to those people. I told them about my years as a drunk and how God saved me. I read them Romans 10:9,10. Then I turned to verses 14,15: ''How then shall they call on him in whom they have not believed? and how shall they believe in him of whom they have not heard? and how shall they hear without a preacher? and how shall they preach unless they be sent?''

''Praise God, I've been sent! You listen to me, brothers. All right, Big Ed?''

''All right, preacher boy, you go right ahead.''

When I was through with my message I told Big Ed that I was going out into the street.

''Grizzly, you go with him,'' Big Ed ordered. Grizzly's appearance matched his name. Now I felt really safe! The Lord had given me Big Ed's protection.

I must have gone to thirty or forty people that night. I preached to drunks everywhere—lying on the ground, in doorways and alleys, under parked cars. I would lift up their heads and ask them, "Do you know Jesus?" They would stutter and stammer in a drunken stupor, but I would share my testimony with them just as I had done with the unconscious man in that hotel doorway in Adelaide.

I let Grizzly go first. Nobody came near me—it was as if I had a ring of fire around me. "Big Ed says nobody hurts this man," Grizzly announced wherever we went.

The following evening after I returned from speaking, I again looked out of my room window. There was the neon sign still blinking.

"You better get moving, Wild Bill."

"Right on, Lord, here I go."

I changed my clothes and descended to the street again. Big Ed was in the bar, dealing the dope. A heavy-set woman came in. She had a terribly scarred face with a droopy eye. She looked awful. Around her neck hung a chain with a tin cup on the end of it into which liquor was poured for her. Her name was Irene, and she talked with a lisp. She wore all her clothes at the same time. She had been burned in a fire and everyone made fun of her. She was known as "Crazy Irene," and was the town character.

"You're Wild Bill," she said. "Big Ed the Moose says we can't touch you."

I turned to Big Ed. "I've been preaching to all these people around here, Big Ed, now how about you? Isaiah 55:6,7 says, 'Seek the Lord while he may be found, call ye upon him while he is near: Let the wicked forsake his way, and the unrighteous man his thoughts: and let him return unto the Lord, and he will have mercy upon him; and to our God, for he will abundantly pardon.' That's speaking to you, Big Ed. Don't you want to know Jesus?''

"I can't do it, Wild Bill," he answered. "I got too good a deal up here, too many things going for me. But I want to tell you something, preacher boy, you almost got me convinced."

I recalled what King Agrippa said to Paul who had testified to him, "Almost thou persuadest me to be a Christian" (Acts 26:28). I stuck out my hand and said, "Goodbye, Big Ed the Moose. I hope to see you in glory."

"Goodbye, preacher boy."

It was 6:00 a.m. when I crawled into bed. I was just about to fall asleep when the door almost came down. When I opened it, there stood the dirtiest, filthiest human being I had ever seen. He was an Eskimo.

"What do you want?" I asked.

"I want to take a shower."

"Well, go ahead." He certainly needed one. He started to take his clothes off.

"You talked to me last night," he said. "I'm going back to Whitehorse this morning; I don't want to live a bad life any longer. I've got a new man in my heart, like you said; I got Jesus down here. I'm a new man! I got white horse in here—black horse gone."

After he had showered, I asked him, "Brother, do you want any clean underwear?"

"No, I don't use it."

"How about some of my clothes? I have some suits that will fit you."

"No, I'm going to go back like I came."

In my heart I shot up an arrow prayer. "This time

I know it's from You, Lord.''

I reached out to get my Bible. "Brother, here's my Bible. I want you to have it.''

He pointed over my shoulder. I looked at the spot he was pointing to and there lay the brand new white Bible I had just been given.

"I want a white Bible,'' he said. "It's new. I never had anything new.''

I took off the cellophane wrapper and wrote on the fly leaf, "Wild Bill Monteith, a child of the King. Romans 10:9,10.''

He reached into those dirty clothes of his and handed me something. "I ain't got nothin' to give you, Wild Bill, but these two things. Here's a walrus whisker and a seal's tooth; they're all I have. I give them to you, now I have nothin'. But you gave me somethin' last night no man can take away. You gave me Jesus.''

"I can't take these things from you,'' I told him, overwhelmed by his act of humble gratitude.

"You take them, and think of me,'' he insisted.

"Okay, I'll do that.'' I took the walrus whisker and the seal's tooth, then watched him leave my room, cross the street, and stand on the bridge over the Cheena River where the Alcan Highway begins its 1,523-mile journey to Dawson. A car stopped to offer him a ride and he climbed in. He was wearing the same old clothes, but inside he was a completely new person. "Therefore if any man be in Christ, he is a new creature: old things are passed away; behold, all things are become new'' (2 Cor. 5:17). Underneath his arm was my beautiful new Bible with the words inscribed on the fly leaf, "Wild Bill Monteith, a child of the King. Romans 10:9,10.''

I still had my black Bible—but not for long.

A short time later, a little guy about four-foot-eleven wandered into the place we were meeting in Santa Ana, California. He looked like a jockey. I knew intuitively that he had come in to ask for money. Before he could say a word, I jumped in. ''I want to talk to you, brother,'' I said, inviting him into the room.

As I was talking to him, the Lord whispered, *''Your Bible.''*

''Lord, I'm not going to give this guy my Bible. I don't even like him. Besides, I've only had that Bible for three months and I just got it all marked up.''

''Your Bible.''

I turned to the little fellow and asked him, ''What's your name, brother?''

''Warren,'' he answered.

I picked up my Bible and handed it to him. ''You're giving this to me?'' he asked with a look of astonishment.

''Yes.''

''No one ever gave me anything before!''

''Well, the Lord asked me to give you my Bible.''

''You know what I was going to do?'' he owned up. ''I was going to ask you for some money. But I'm not going to do that now. This is the only gift anybody has ever given me. I'm from Detroit and I'm going back there.'' He hesitated, still amazed by the gift. ''Can I really have this?''

''You sure can,'' I assured him. With that, we parted.

I knew that the Holy Spirit had brought Warren into that building so I could sow a seed which someone else would water. I could picture him somewhere on the road between California and Detroit, carrying my Bible, with the words on the fly leaf which I wrote in all my Bibles. I prayed that as he read the stories between the covers of that Bible the Lord would touch his heart, and He would send someone along to bring the seed to maturity and harvest.

"There is an appointed time for everything. And there is a time for every event under heaven," we are told in the *New American Standard* version of Ecclesiastes 3:1. There is a time to sow, a time to water, and a time to harvest. I have been used to do all three of these things in my life.

I had been very persistent with the girl on my flight to Anchorage—the Holy Spirit had revealed to me how I was to reach her. With many of the drunks in the bars and on the streets of Fairbanks I had merely sown a seed. One Eskimo's soul I had harvested. With Warren, I had planted. I am sure that I must have watered seed in some hearts which had been planted there earlier by someone else.

But whether it is sowing, watering or harvesting, the important thing is that we be faithful witnesses of the saving grace of the Lord Jesus Christ. We don't have to beat anybody over the head with the Gospel; we just have to be sensitive to the openings the Holy Spirit provides for us, ministering in the manner in which He prompts us.

There is no formula for bringing souls into the Kingdom of God. Sometimes we only get to put the first piece of the jigsaw puzzle on the board. Some puzzles require a lot of pieces. At times we put an important piece in along the way and it forms a link for many other pieces to fall together. And sometimes we have the joy of seeing the picture complete.

Wherever I go, whomever I meet, I am constantly aware that God has me where I am for a reason. He has the blueprint for my life, and He knows where He wants me, even though I may not see how a word here or a Bible given away there fits into the big picture.

"Therefore, we are ambassadors for Christ, as though God were entreating through us," we are told in 2 Corinthians 5:20 (NAS). An ambassador doesn't decide where to go or what to say—he is sent. Today, God will send you into someone's life. Listen for the prompting of His Spirit. No matter how small a role you may appear to play, it's all part of His master plan. A smile, a kind word, passing a tract to someone, leaving a copy of *Voice* magazine in a telephone booth; whatever it may be, respond to what God tells you to do.

Someday, we will all be amazed at how the Lord has used us—at the role we played in bringing a child of God into the Kingdom. Jesus said, "'He who is faithful in a very little thing is faithful also in much; and he who is unrighteous in a very little thing is unrighteous also in much'" (Luke 16:10 NAS). Be a faithful ambassador in the little things, and watch how much God will do through them.

7

An Epitaph

I didn't want to go to Nebraska; I would have much preferred to stay home. But there's one question the Christian must continually ask himself: "Am I where God wants me to be?"

It was 2:30 a.m. Mavis and I were sound asleep in our hotel room in Scottsbluff, Nebraska. Room 727. There was no bolt on the door, just the regular lock.

Suddenly the door burst open and in barged a guy wearing a huge sombrero and sporting a large mustache.

"What are you doing in here?" I asked with alarm.

"What do you mean, 'What am I doing in here'?" he retorted.

"This is *my* room," I said indignantly.

"No it isn't," he countered, "it's *my* room."

"What room key have you got?" I demanded.

"727."

I dialed the desk. "Hey, there's somebody in my room."

"What room are you in?"

"727."

"What's your name?"

"Bill Monteith."

"You can't be, you checked out."

"No I didn't. I'm still here."

There was a pause while the desk clerk checked the computer. Then he announced, "The computer says you checked out."

"I don't care what your computer says, I say I'm

still here. I'm going to send this other guy down to the desk and you give him another room," I said.

I heard the clerk tell someone, "There's a really weird guy in room 727."

I'm not weird, I'm peculiar. All God's people are peculiar.

The instant the sun came up over the Scottsbluff mountains Mavis announced, "I want to get out of here." We got into our rental car and headed toward Oshkosh, Nebraska, where we stopped for breakfast. When we got back into the car again and started down the road, a drunk pulled out right in front of us. He was veering from one lane to the other; I wanted to get past him but I couldn't. So Mavis sent up one of her arrow prayers: "Lord, have an officer come because this man's under the influence of alcohol." We could see that he had a wife and two little children in the car with him.

Suddenly we heard a siren. There was a car behind me as well as the drunk in front of me. The policeman stopped them both, so I tried to pull out around them and go on. The policeman stood in the middle of the highway, blocking my path, and shouted at me: "You! Stop, and pull over!"

I said, "Me?"

"You! Over!"

He went to the driver behind me and gave him a ticket; then he went to the drunk, but he didn't smell his breath. In a minute he waved him on! I couldn't believe it. Finally he came back to me.

"Goin' kinda fast, weren't you?"

"No, I wasn't going very fast, I was keeping right at the speed limit," I said innocently. He started writing and in a minute he handed me a warning ticket.

"You were exceeding the speed limit. You're from out of state. If you are caught speeding in the state of Nebraska again, you are going to get the book thrown at you."

"Yes sir," I said politely, venturing to ask, "How fast was I going?"

"You were going 57 in a 55-mile zone," he snapped.

"Oh, I am a criminal, am I?" I chuckled.

"No," he said, "but that's going too fast."

My car didn't have cruise control so in my effort to avoid the drunk driver I had accidentally drifted two miles per hour over the speed limit. An airplane, checking the speed of all three cars, had radioed ahead to the patrol car to stop us.

It was turning out to be one of those trips, full of such annoying little incidents which can spoil your whole day if you let them. I really hadn't wanted to make this trip in the first place, and there were plenty of little irritations to lend support to my preconceived skepticism about it. I had little desire to fly into Denver, pick up a car, and drive twenty-four hundred miles visiting such metropolises as North Loop City, population 323. We took a picture of one hotel we stayed in. Inside it looked like it was snowing! But it wasn't snow, it was the wallpaper peeling off. It was the oldest hotel I have ever seen in my life, and I honestly didn't care to stay there. But unfortunately there was no choice; it was the only lodging available in the place we were ministering.

Our last night was spent in North Platte. We were staying at the Holiday Inn, which was normally a very nice place in which to get some rest. But not *this* trip!

Since we were both totally bushed from the long

day's drive and the lack of sleep from the night before, as soon as we got checked in we lay down on the bed for a rest. It was about ninety-six degrees. At that moment the air conditioner went out. Then the lights went out. Next minute we heard a siren in the distance. As it drew closer and closer, Mavis began to pray in tongues.

I looked out of the hotel door and there was a fire engine, followed by a second, then a third. "I think there's a fire," I announced.

"Shall I get dressed?" Mavis inquired.

I opened the door wider and walked out. The lady in the next room came out too. "Are you evacuating the building?" she asked.

"No, I don't think so."

"Well," she said, "the place is on fire."

"How do you know?" I asked.

"Look at all that smoke," she answered. It was true, there was a lot of smoke. When I called the front desk I learned that there was an electrical fire in the hotel kitchen and the fire brigade was spraying foam on it.

When I returned to the room Mavis was dressed and in her hands she held two Bibles, nothing else. (I could tell what was important in her life!) As we walked outside and around to the front of the hotel, we couldn't help but notice the message on the marquee: "Welcome, Nebraska Fire Prevention Association." You can be sure we took a picture of that!

I hadn't wanted to come to Nebraska; I would have much preferred to stay home. But there is only one question I must always ask myself: "Am I where God wants me to be?"

It doesn't matter how difficult or unpleasant the

circumstances may be. It doesn't matter how impossible the situation may seem. If I am where God wants me to be, He will not fail me. No matter how crushing the burden may be which I have to bear, no matter how much suffering or pain I may have to endure, I can be at peace and rest when I know that God is with me.

If I am where God wants me to be, He will work a direct miracle if necessary rather than allow me to perish from lack. The manna always accompanies the pillar of cloud. All I have to do is rest in the Lord and wait patiently for Him, no matter how desolate my surroundings, how bleak my prospects.

When Elijah closed up the heavens in the land of Israel, God fed him by the brook Cherith. (1 Kings 17:1-7.) Eventually the waters of the brook began to dry up. God's servants are often called to sit by a drying brook. It may be the drying brook of health as we see ourselves sinking under a creeping paralysis or cancer. It may be the drying brook of finances as the money slowly dwindles away and a pile of unpaid bills mounts. It may be the drying brook of popularity, where we find ourselves taking a course in life that is increasingly unpopular and which meets with disapproval from our peers. Or it may be the drying brook of friendship, so that we find ourselves losing former friends and are left alone with only God as our companion.

Why does God let the brooks dry up?

Because He wants to drain us of all self-reliance so that we abandon ourselves to Him. He demands our implicit trust, regardless of outer circumstances. He has to know that we will cling to Him come what may. As Job said of God when his brooks began to run dry: "Though he slay me, yet will I trust in him" (Job

13:15). We must learn to trust God absolutely.

While Elijah dwelt by the brook Cherith he was alone with God. God's servants must be taught the value of the hidden life. We cannot give out unless we have first taken in. Before beginning his ministry, Paul retired to the Arabian desert, there to prepare himself for spiritual combat. It was while John was secluded in a Roman prison on the island of Patmos that God gave him the Revelation of Jesus Christ. Our Lord found His Cherith in Nazareth, in the wilderness of Judea, amid the olive trees of Bethany, and in the solitude of Gadara.

Before He can remove us to some other sphere of service, God has to loosen our roots. This "root loosening" may take many different forms. Perhaps circumstances don't work out the way we had planned. We may become less attached to a home, a job, a certain set of friends, a particular church group.

Only when the streams had dwindled to pools, and the pools to drops, and the drops to sand—only then did the word of the Lord come to Elijah telling him, "Arise, get thee to Zarephath, which belongeth to Zidon, and dwell there: behold, I have commanded a widow woman there to sustain thee" (1 Kings 17:9).

We are told simply that Elijah "arose and went" (v. 10). When God takes me home to be with Him, I want three things to be inscribed on my tombstone: the date I was born, the date I died, and the inscription, "He arose and went."

I want to be ready to go wherever God sends me. I don't care how much He has to loosen the soil around my roots, or how dry my brook has to become in order to prepare me for the work He has for me to do. I don't relish difficulties and trials, but it's far more important that I be made ready for God's use than it is that I have a comfortable existence.

Whenever I have gone where God wanted me to go, I have experienced the wonderful blessing of seeing people helped. There is no greater reward than to see lives changed because we had an impact upon them. That's why I always want to be available, even though I may not always feel like it.

We had a glorious meeting in North Platte. Afterwards one of the brothers came to me and said, "Hey, Wild Bill, there's a man playing piano in the hotel bar who was saved about two years ago in one of our meetings, but now he's back out there in the world."

"Have you fellows been to see him?" I inquired.

"Oh, no, he's in the bar!" they answered, sounding shocked.

"Well, what difference does that make?" I asked.

"But Christians aren't supposed to go into bars," they protested.

"Are you kidding?" I responded. "I go wherever the least, the lost and the last live!"

The brother's name was Mike. I went to the bar and passed him a note: "Mike, Jesus loves you."

When the note reached him, he picked it up and stared at it for a while; then he asked, "Is this a request for a song, or does somebody have a message for me?"

"Brother," I responded from the audience, "I have a message for you." He came over to where I was sitting and I told him, "Mike, I came into the bar just to tell you that Jesus loves you and I love you. I'm sorry that the brothers have not been to see you. I usually check the bars out before our meetings, but I didn't know about you until afterwards."

"Brother, can you stay and talk to me?" he asked.

"Of course," I replied, "that's why I'm here."

I went to get Mavis and when we returned Mike began to pour out his heart to us. He told us that he had been saved in a bar and was Spirit-filled. He said that he had tried his best to stay out of sin, but that his playmates had dragged him back into the world. Now he was so under condemnation for slipping back into the world that he hadn't used his prayer language in over a year.

I put my arms around this brother and began to pray in tongues. As I did so, his own prayer language was revived and he started to praise the Lord. Then a girl who was in his band came over. I had spoken in North Loop City and her mother had happened to be there. She had told her daughter that I was going to be in North Platte. It was a beautiful time of sharing.

What concerned me most was the fact that here were brothers attending a Christian meeting in a downtown hotel, yet they hadn't taken time out to check the hotel bar. I always do that. I ask the bartender for a Holy Spirit cocktail, and when he asks me what that is I tell him. Then I invite him to the meeting where we have some real "spirits"!

In Lincoln, Nebraska, as I walked by the bar I noticed a woman in there with a little girl who looked to be about nine years of age. The bartender was sitting with them and they were laughing. I walked up to the lady and inquired, "Is this your daughter?"

"Yes, she is," she answered.

"What is she doing in here sitting at the bar?" I demanded.

At that juncture the bartender chimed in, "She only has a Shirley Temple cocktail."

"I didn't ask you," I said, putting him in his place,

"I asked her mother." Again I demanded, "What's your little daughter doing in here drinking?"

"It's only a Shirley Temple," she replied, "and there's no harm in that."

At that point I lit into her. "I don't care what happens to you, lady; but that little girl of yours is only about nine years of age. I'm going to tell you something. Either you get your daughter out of here or something very violent is going to happen to you. God is going to strike you! Your life may be already over with, but that little girl has an opportunity to grow up clean. You take her home, do you understand me?"

They stared at me in amazement. I think the bartender wanted to throw me out; but when you have the Holy Spirit surrounding you, you have an impenetrable shield. The little girl's mother answered apologetically, "Yes, sir. I'll go right now," and she left.

The bartender looked at me as if he was about to say something, so I jumped in ahead of him. "The next time you do that, God is going to come down and get you too!" With that, I walked out.

There is a time to confront evil. I'm not saying that we have to go out looking for people to accost. Elijah didn't go out in search of those who were perpetrating evil in his day, they were all around him. But when God instructed him to do something about it, he was not afraid to confront the king and queen themselves.

Things were pretty dark in Israel around that time. After the death of Solomon his kingdom was split into two factions, with Rehoboam taking the southern part and Jeroboam the northern. Jeroboam had been superintendent of Solomon's vast array of public works. When he took control of the north, he was afraid that the people might be wooed back to the south because they had to go up to Jerusalem to the annual feasts. To circumvent this, he built an altar in the north of his kingdom at Dan, and another on his southern border at Bethel. He was the worst king who had lived in Israel to that time. (1 Kings 14:7-9.)

Later on, Ahab became king of Israel; and like his predecessors, he too "did more to provoke the Lord God of Israel to anger than all the kings of Israel that were before him" (1 Kings 17:33). One of the evil things Ahab did was to take as his wife, Jezebel—the daughter of a pagan king—who influenced Ahab to join her in worshipping Baal. (1 Kings 17:31.) This Jezebel was a crafty, unscrupulous, cruel woman—a Phoenician—who used her husband as a tool for her own selfish schemes. When God commanded Elijah to go to this wicked royal couple and speak out against them, it took a great deal of courage. Elijah was well aware of their power and cruelty. He knew what might happen to him if he opposed them. But God protected him because he was obedient to his Lord's commands. God will always go with us when He sends us to confront evil.

Maggie and George are special friends of ours. Their son, Rick, is a great baseball player. He is so good that he was awarded an athletic scholarship to attend college. He was leading the team in batting; in fact, he had more home runs to his credit than the rest of the team members combined.

Rick's coach had a filthy mouth and constantly used the name of God in vain. The day dawned when Rick couldn't stand it anymore. He went up to the coach on the field and said, "Sir, I'm a Christian. Would you please not use the name of my Lord in vain?"

As a result of his action, Rick was benched for three weeks. Each night he went home and cried, asking God, "Lord, did I do right to stand up for You?" It had cost him dearly to honor the name of Christ.

After the three weeks, Mavis and I joined together with Rick's parents in fervent prayer for his situation. After that, Rick was allowed to play again, and in his first game he scored two home runs. But he wasn't allowed enough times at bat during the season. So when the professional major league teams made their draft lists, Rick's name was not included. Instead he was sent to a semi-pro league for college boys in Lincoln, Nebraska.

Rick was bitter toward the Lord—so bitter that when he packed to leave home for Nebraska he didn't even take his Bible. He was like Elijah in 1 Kings 19 when Jezebel sent a messenger to tell him that she would kill him. Faced with that threat, Elijah arose and fled for his life all the way to Beersheba, the southernmost part of Israel. There the lord met him and instructed him to go forty days to Mount Horeb, where he hid in a cave.

There is no cave so deep and dark, no spot on earth so lonely, that the word of the Lord cannot come to us. It is impossible to escape from God. He came to Elijah in that solitary place and asked him what he was doing there. Elijah poured out his bitterness: "Lord, I'm here by myself—there's nobody else out there. Everybody is bowing down to idols. They've erected groves, they've slain the prophets. I'm the only one left to represent You, so I had to run for my life because they were going to kill me too.''

At that moment the Lord passed by. Elijah looked out of the cave and watched the devastation which occurred as a mighty wind brought down great rocks and split them. Then an earthquake split the mountain, followed by a fire which burned the dry tufts of grass and scorched all the trees. But Got was not to be found in the wind, earthquake or fire. After all of this display of force, God came to Elijah. He was in the still, small voice—that voice from which no man can escape, as much as he may try to block it out.

The Lord told Elijah that there were still seven thousand in Israel who had not bowed their knees to Baal. But where were those seven thousand ''closet believers'' whom Elijah didn't even know about? Who were they? Elijah was the prophet; if anybody could tell who belonged to the Lord and who didn't, it should have been Elijah. In Ahab's own household there was a chief steward, Obadiah, who knew the Lord; he had hidden a hundred prophets of the Lord in a cave. But it seems that Elijah didn't know about him.

Many believers are like that. They are ''secret service Christians''—''closet Christians.'' There are scores of Obadiahs in our churches today, but they never show their true colors. They find pretexts and excuses to avoid having to take a stand for Christ and to lessen the guilt of their uneasy conscience. They are sorry for those who do take a stand for the Lord and suffer persecution for righteousness; but it never occurs to these people to stand in the pillory by their side. Somehow they just can't seem to muster the courage to step out boldly and declare their true allegiance. Rather than spread the Word themselves, many modern-day Christians would rather have some big-name preacher come into town to hold a huge, earth-shaking revival full of sound and fury; but often God is not in the earthquake, wind or fire.

When we were in Lincoln, Nebraska, Mavis and I took Rick out to dinner. We were supposed to be in York, Nebraska, the next day, but Rick had an evening game that day so we dalayed our departure long enough to meet with him and minister to him. Rick had paddled his canoe upstream for awhile; but when he wasn't drafted into the major leagues, he stopped paddling and began to float downstream with the rest of the world, as so often happens to disappointed Christians.

Rick had been planning to go to a discotheque with some of his friends that evening, but when we showed up he consented to have dinner with us. With the help of the Lord we were able to help Rick regain his sense of purpose and his trust in God's love and provision. We put a paddle back in his hands, and he began to row once again. He had gone to Nebraska angry with God, but now he was reconciled with his Lord and ready to begin again, confident that all things do work together for good to those who love the Lord and who are the called according to His purpose.

When I realized the impact of our visit upon Rick's life, I was so glad that we hadn't stayed home—that we had been obedient to go where God sent us.

It's not always easy to be a Christian; we sometimes have to put up with a lot of abuse. You should hear what some of my ex-friends call me when I occasionally bump into them. But I don't care. I know what I was, I know what I am, and I know where I am going.

"He arose and went." Will your posterity honestly be able to inscribe those words on *your* tombstone? I can think of no greater epitaph.

When Isaiah saw a vision of the Lord, he said: "I heard the voice of the Lord, saying, Whom shall I send, and who will go for us? Then said I, Here am I; send me" (Is. 6:8). I want God to send me. I want to be ready when He has a job that he needs me to do. If that means I have to sit by a few drying brooks, so be it. I want to know God as my total supply in every circumstance of life. May I never allow any obstacle to prevent me from faithfully carrying out the mission which He has sent me to accomplish.

No matter what the cost, the persecution, the discomfort, the inconvenience, the hardship—I want God to be able to say of Wild Bill, "He arose and went."

8

Steve Doesn't Live Here Anymore

There's hardly a family in America which hasn't been touched by the problem of the "prodigal son." Mine was no exception. At age eighteen, my son Steve was gone. What do you do if your son or daughter has strayed? How do you cope if they are into drugs, alcohol, or living an immoral life? God has an answer, and it works. My son is back home!

When our flight touched down in San Francisco the stewardess suggested that we leave the plane for a short break before continuing on the second leg of our journey to Spokane, Washington. Before deplaning I placed an "occupied" sign on my window seat.

San Francisco is one of the three cities in the world with the spirit of homosexuality over them; the other two are Amsterdam and Sydney. Those three cities have more homosexuality than any others in the world. Since there was a little time before our flight continued, I thought perhaps I would set foot in the devil's workshop and take the opportunity to pray for the city.

After our short layover I reboarded the plane and sauntered casually down the aisle toward my seat. I had selected a window seat because I hadn't been to Spokane for a long time and I wanted to see the beautiful green of the countryside in contrast to the brown and smog of Southern California.

When I arrived at my seat I discovered that a lady was sitting in it, despite my clearly displayed "occupied" sign. I didn't want to say anything to her myself, since I'm a gentleman; besides, I was sporting my Full Gospel Business Men's Fellowship pin. So

I walked down the aisle to the stewardess and announced, "There's a lady in my seat."

"I know," she said.

"Well, I had an 'occupied' sign on it," I persisted. "I got off the plane to stretch my legs like you told me to, and now she's in my seat. What are you going to do about it?"

"There were only two seats vacant," the stewardess explained, "and she has her little daughter with her. By letting her take your seat she is able to have her little daughter sit with her. Now you wouldn't want her to have to sit all alone, would you?"

"No, I don't mind giving up my seat," I answered. "Do you have any other seats?" I made myself sound gracious, but inside I didn't feel gracious. "That is my seat!" I told myself. "I want to look out the window at all the trees!"

I followed the stewardess up and down the aisle. "Is this seat taken?"

"Yes."

"Is that seat taken?"

"Yes."

About the time I was beginning to think I was going to have to stand up all the way to Spokane the stewardess announced triumphantly, "I found one!" Then she promptly put me in a middle seat. Now if there's one thing I hate it's the middle seat on an aircraft. I like the aisle seat or the window seat, but here I was in the middle.

To install myself in the seat I had to climb over a huge hunk of a guy who made Rosey Grier look like a midget. He was a giant. His arms were like fence posts, his hands like catcher's mitts, and his fingers looked like Oscar Meyer weiners. His muscles rippled out over half my seat. The guy on the other side was more normal sized, but he was stretched out asleep, so his elbow was jammed into my ribs.

I noticed that the giant was reading *Sports Illustrated*. I like to talk when I am on an airplane, but since he looked too big to tangle with, I took out my Bible and the issue of *Voice* magazine that had my testimony in it. Finally I worked up the courage to ask him, "Are you a Christian?"

"I go to church," he answered.

"Going to church doesn't make you a Christian any more than going into a garage makes you an automobile," I explained. He didn't seem to catch on at all so I continued. "Let me explain it again. I know you say you go to church, but there's a difference between going to church and being a Christian."

"Well, I just got married last week," he retorted. What the connection was supposed to be between getting married and being a Christian, I didn't know.

"I've been married for twenty-eight years," I said, "and I'll pray for your marriage. But you're still not following me. Let me say it again: knowing the Lord Jesus has come into your heart is a lot different from going to church or getting married. Would you like to read my testimony?"

He hesitated, looking at me as if I was weird, so I shoved it in front of him and said, "Read it. See that picture? That's me. Read it."

"Okay, I'll read it, I'll read it!"

"Don't skip any of it," I added bravely. "Read it all the way through because when you get through I'm going to give you a quiz on it."

He began to read. After he had finished the article I asked, "Well, how did you like it?"

''That's really neat,'' he said, ''that's nice for you.''

''What do you do,'' I asked.

''I'm a football coach. My name's John. I was an offensive line coach at a college in California. Our team used to play in the Rose Bowl. But when the head coach accepted a job with the pros I was out of a job. I'm on my way now up to Washington state to a new coaching position; my wife's already there.''

''Well, John, it's really nice to have a new wife and a new job, but let's talk about your soul,'' I picked up. ''You know, the Lord really loves you.''

I laid it on him hard. I talked about how I came to the Lord, and how my boys had been on drugs but how the Lord had delivered them.

''I'm royalty, a joint-heir with Jesus Christ, with all the rights and privileges that go with it,'' I explained. ''All I did was read Romans 10:9,10 and believe it, and this is what happened to me.'' Then I quoted the passage to him.

''That's neat,'' he said.

''You know, we have something in common, you and I. I like sports too. When I was living in the world, I used to go to the Rose Bowl a lot. In fact, I've probably been there more times than you have. The only difference is, I was always in a drunken stupor when I went. Can you imagine the Lord finding me when I was in that condition, saving me, and delivering me from booze—all in one fell swoop?''

''That's pretty incredible,'' he admitted. Then he began to share more about his life. After a while his eyes began to fill up with tears. ''I like what you say,'' he added. I could sense the Spirit of the Lord moving upon him.

"Well, why don't we go through the sinner's prayer together?" I suggested.

"Right now?"

"Right now. If you'll just give me a little room here to move, I'll open my Bible."

So, seven miles up in the air we went through the sinner's prayer, and he meant every word of it. He was sick and tired of being sick and tired; he wanted to start out his new marriage, his new job and his new life feeling right. By the time we had finished praying he was glorying in the Lord, basking in joy, crying and laughing, reveling in tongues. The stewardess couldn't figure out what he was saying—she thought he was asking for a 7-Up!

I turned to the guy on my other side, who by this time was awake and had removed his elbow from my ribs. "Are you saved?" I asked.

"I just heard what you said to the brother there," he answered. "I've been saved a long time."

"Praise the Lord, brother!"

"But when you talked about your boys . . . " He started to say something, then abruptly added, "Oh, I don't want to talk about it."

"Come on, talk about it," I urged. "We've got a long way to go; we're just out of San Francisco."

"Well, I'm an attorney in Montana. I just came from San Francisco and I have to go back and tell my wife something terrible."

"What do you have to say to her, brother?"

"I live in a small town outside of Billings. I have the only law practice in town—I inherited it from my father. I have a son and he was always a straight-A student. After he finished high school we sent him to the University of California. He was on the Dean's List

127

as a freshman. But then he went back last year as a sophomore and we didn't hear from him. We wrote him letter after letter, but he never wrote back. We became worried when we couldn't reach him by phone, so we called the university and were told that he had dropped out of school."

"That's too bad," I sympathized. I could feel his pain. Today I have three beautiful sons who all know the Lord. Two of them are in the ministry. Jeff never left home and today he has a lovely wife called Cindy. Louie also stayed home, marrying his beautiful wife Cheryl. But one of my sons did leave home. God uses all of the tragedies we go through in life to help others when we love Him and allow Him to flow through us. I was beginning to see why He had let me get sandwiched between these two men instead of enjoying the view out of my window seat.

The lawyer continued. "I went to San Francisco to find my boy. I had an address; we had sent him money. He was in a place down by the wharf, the sleaziest place I have ever seen. When I walked up to it the door was open, and inside I found my son with a woman who was old enough to be his mother. He was unshaven, drunk, and high on dope.

"'What's wrong with you, son?' I asked him.

"'Hey, man, don't bother me,' he told me. 'I've got my own life to live, man. I'm really enjoying it.'

"The place reeked of marijuana and the woman was so glassy-eyed that she couldn't even talk to me; she sat there having a conversation with the stove.

"'Gary, come on back home,' I urged.

"'Man, I'm not coming back home,' he told me, 'I've really got it made here. I'm happy. First time in my life I've really been happy. Now shove off, man.'

"My heart was broken as I walked down the stairs. I got on this airplane and then I heard you talking about your three boys, and how God reached out to them when they were on drugs. In my heart I was asking, 'Why doesn't God do something for me?'"

"Hey, brother," I interjected, "I want to tell you that God *can* do something for your boy. We've got about thirty minutes left; let me tell you what He did for my family."

"Okay, I'll listen," he agreed.

I began to relate how God had brought my son back home. "I was at our church in Orange County," I explained, "when a man came up to me whom I hadn't seen in twenty-five years. He was an old friend from college days.

"'Wild Bill,' he said, 'what are *you* doing in church?'

"I asked him equally increduously, 'What are *you* doing in church?' The last time I had seen him he was almost as big a drunk as I had been; the only difference between us was that he drank Scotch while I preferred bourbon.

"'Brother, I'm saved,' he said.

"'Well, I'm saved too,' I told him. 'And filled with the Holy Spirit.'

"'Oh, I'm so excited,' he exclaimed, 'I didn't think . . . I mean, I thought everybody could be saved but you, Wild Bill!'

"I introduced him to my wife, Mavis, then I said, 'I'd like to introduce you to my boy, Jeff. He's my eldest and he's graduated from Melodyland School of Theology. He's going to be a pastor and teacher. He used to pump himself full of drugs, but now He's filled with the Spirit.'

"'And here's my youngest boy, Louie. He is going to Southern California College—that's an Assembly of God college—and he has a ministry in music. He loves the Lord and he's going to write songs. We have a beautiful family.'

"'Wild Bill, I thought you said you had three sons,' he said.

"'Steve is the one in between,' I explained, 'but Steve is eighteen years old and he doesn't live with us anymore. I can't tell you the exact day or hour when he started building a wall against his mom and dad, but it happened somewhere around four or five years ago. There came a day when he put in the final brick that stopped communication between parents and son. He left home in his mind a long time before he left physically. There were a lot of tears, a lot of heartaches, and a great many disappointments.

"'Then on July 9 last year he told me he was going to leave home—said he wanted to get his head together and would probably never come home again. He reached out his hand to say goodbye and I took him in my arms. The tears rolled down my face and splattered on the floor as he told me something that he hadn't told me since the Christmas he got his creepy-crawlers set. He told me that he loved me, and I told him that I loved him too. I don't remember telling him that all during the time he was rebelling against us in junior and senior high school. There was never a kind word between Steve and me then, just rebellion on his part and anger and frustration on mine; but before he left home God gave me the opportunity to put my arms around him and tell him that I loved him.'

"So Steve wasn't with us when I met my old college buddy," I explained to my traveling companion.

"But since then God has done some wonderful things and I want to share them with you because I believe He can do the same for you and your son."

The lawyer was listening intently, deeply moved by my parallel experience to what he was now going through.

"We have a large picture window at home," I continued, "and we watched Steve leave in an old beat-up station wagon with all his earthly possessions—a TV set and stereo, a fishing pole, and a Planters Peanuts wastebasket. We live across from a park so we could watch him drive away for some distance.

"That day Mavis and I kneeled in our home and claimed three Scriptures that God had given us. We burned them into our hearts and we stood on them. Every night we would kneel beside our bed and claim them. The first is Jeremiah 31:16 where God promises that our weeping will not be in vain for our children will return from the land of the enemy. The second is Acts 16:31 which says that our whole household will be saved. In the Jewish nation at that time a person's household included not only his immediate family but also his relatives, including his parents. We claimed that one for our whole family, especially my seventy-nine-year-old mother. The third Scripture was Joshua 24:15. Like Joshua we claimed God's promise that our whole house would serve the Lord. It didn't look like those promises would ever be honored at the time. Steve had gone into a life of drugs."

Our plane had begun its descent into Spokane as I related how I am usually the first to arise in the morning and how one morning I was praying in the Spirit when I happened to glance out of our picture window and see a tall, gangly youth with a huge mop of unruly hair coming across the park. I didn't notice who he was, but as he reached the Little League field half-way across the park my spirit left my body. I found myself over in the Little League field, and there I was with my arms around a little thirteen-year-old boy. It was Steve, and he had just lost his Little League baseball game and was crying. That's the last time I could remember having my arms around him and doing anything with him before he went into rebellion.

"Suddenly I was back in the room praying in the Spirit again," I related, "and by now my face was wet with perspiration; I was really travailing in prayer. I saw this figure again and he was wearing a gray Mickey Mouse shirt, a pair of tan cords, and was barefoot; now he was at the curb on the street.

"'My goodness, that's Steve,' I said to myself, 'and he's come home!'

"The story of the prodigal son flashed to mind, where the father rushes out to meet his son; he doesn't wait for him to come in. So I ran across the living room, opened the door, and raced across the patio to open the big iron gate. Just as I ran across the lawn I felt the Lord's hand upon me and I heard a voice saying, 'It's not time, Wild Bill; it's not time.' I looked up and nobody was in the park. Steve wasn't there—nobody was there. It had been a vision.

"Mavis and I continued to pray. We knew that the day was going to come when God would fulfill His promises. It was on October 10 that I heard a knock at the door, and when I opened it there stood a tall gangly youth wearing a gray Mickey Mouse shirt, a pair of tan cords—and he was barefoot. It was Steve, and he had come home! My brothers and sisters had joined with me in prayer and God had put a hook in

Steve's mouth sixteen hundred miles away and had drawn him back home.

"There were wounds to heal on both sides; there was an abrasiveness to be smoothed out. But the day came when the same preacher who had led me to Christ stood at the altar of that same Baptist church.

On one side of him stood my son Jeff, as best man. On the other side, as usher, stood Louie. Then down the aisle came a tall, gangly lad still with that mop of unruly hair. But this time he didn't have on a Mickey Mouse shirt and tan cords—he was wearing a tuxedo. Steve and Camille were married in that church, and as Mavis and I sat in the front pew, the Spirit of God came upon us and we began to weep.

"You see, I wrote my name on that Baptist church roof the day I was saved, December 11, 1970, and I am a King's kid with all of the rights and privileges that go with that position. So God answers my prayers. He not only gave back my sons, but today I have two beautiful granddaughters named Jill and Amy and a fine grandson named Robert Steven."

As I finished my story, the lawyer began to weep. "Wild Bill, that's exactly what I needed to hear. I was really dreading having to go home and face my wife with the terrible news about our son. I knew it would practically kill her. Now I can bring her hope and assurance instead of grief and despair."

"Brother," I told him, "I want to pray with both you and John."

John reached over with a huge paw to clench one of my hands, while I held on to the lawyer's hand with the other. Together the three of us asked the Lord's blessing on these two men. We asked God to clean up that boy in San Francisco. We prayed that God would prepare his mother's heart for the news, that she would not harbor any animosity or fear but that she would trust Him to work out all things for good for all concerned.

When we stepped off the plane in Spokane the lawyer had to run and catch another flight, but before he left all three of us hugged each other as people stood by and watched. It turned out that this man had never been hugged by another man before, so it meant a great deal to him. How glad I was that the lady and her little girl had taken my window seat!

I don't know how many fathers and mothers reading this book have prodigal sons or daughters, but it's a gigantic problem in this generation. My son, Steve, left home in his mind and his feelings a long time before he left physically. You may have a child in your home who hasn't left yet, but who is every bit as much a prodigal as mine was.

When was the last time you put your arms around your sons or your daughters and told them that you love them? How much time do you spend communicating with them? Not talking at them or preaching to them, but listening to them and being sure that you are really hearing them?

If you have a son or daughter who has left home, Jesus can bring that child back again. But you are going to have to put your hook into him or her through prayer.

In Luke 18:1-8 Jesus told a parable about a judge who neither feared God nor respected man. A widow who knew her rights kept coming to him asking for the legal protection she was due. It was only her continual coming to him that moved the judge to action. Jesus concluded, ''And shall not God avenge his own elect, which cry day and night unto him, though he bear long with them? I tell you that he will avenge them speedily. Nevertheless when the Son of man cometh, shall he find faith on the earth?'' (vv. 7,8).

As an heir of God and joint-heir with Jesus, you have a right to have your family saved. If your children have strayed, God is willing to bring them back. The question is, do you really believe that He can and will do so? Jesus said that the reason we don't receive is because we don't believe. We ask once or twice, but we don't persist.

When my boy left I thought God would bring him home someday, but I didn't really believe He would save him too; I didn't think that was possible. But Mavis and I prayed every night until we believed, and we believed until we received. We stayed with it.

Jesus promised, ''Therefore I say unto you, What things soever ye ask, when ye pray, believe that ye receive them and ye shall have them'' (Mark 11:24). He also said, ''If ye abide in me, and my words abide in you, ye shall ask what ye will, and it shall be done unto you'' (John 15:7).

But there is a condition to answered prayer, and that is to have a forgiving attitude. (Mark 11:25.) When a child leaves home or builds a wall between himself and his parents, the parents will undoubtedly feel very hurt. There will be a temptation to lash out by being judgemental and condemning. Such can only serve to drive the child farther away.

The story Jesus told about the prodigal son speaks directly to this situation. (Luke 15:11-32.) When the younger brother wanted to leave home, the father did not judge him. He accepted his departure as a necessary step in the ultimate salvation of the son. Every mile his son traveled away from home was actually a mile closer to his ultimate reconciliation with his earthly father and his heavenly Father. Although it appeared that the son was going far away, by faith the father knew that he was coming home.

Paramount in any such family crisis is unconditional love. We cannot say to our children, "We will love you if you do such and such." The Bible nowhere allows for conditional love on the part of a Christian. We are to love the just and the unjust, the lovely and the unlovely, those who deserve our love and those who don't. We are to turn the other cheek, to go the extra mile. When we invite only those who are in harmony with us to a banquet, we achieve nothing for the cause of Christ; it is only when we invite the outcasts, the untouchables, the undesirables, that we show love.

At times parents turn their backs on their children and justify such action by saying that "love has to be tough sometimes." But we are hard pressed to find such a definition of love in the love chapter, 1 Corinthians 13. Real love is not "tough," it is unconditional. Love never gives up, never stops being kind, always thinks the best. Even in the face of outright hatred from a child, a loving parent will return only kindness, looking for the good in the child even when there may appear to be none.

Unconditional love is, above all, supportive. Support and confrontation are the two key aspects of a genuine love for another person, but confrontation must always be in the context of support. Only when enough support has been given for the child to know beyond a shadow of a doubt that we truly love, can there ever be confrontation. And by confrontation I do not mean condemnation. For instance, if a teenager is using drugs I do not have to say that such behavior is just fine; I can confront it. If the child wants my opinion of his behavior, I am bound to give it as a loving parent. But I will venture such an opinion only when I have demonstrated full support for the child as a person. I do not have to approve of his actions, but I must approve of him, never turn my back on him, never shut him out.

Most of us have grown up with so much condemnation that we can't take any more. What people need today is not condemnation, but love. They need to know that they are accepted totally. This is how God reaches us, and it is the only way we can reach the person who is in opposition to us. It was while we were yet sinners, still enemies of God, that He gave His own Son to lay down His life for us. That is unconditional love.

Too many parents want to compel their children to live righteous lives. The father of the prodigal never did that. He simply set an example of unconditional love, and trusted that when the son had sown his wild oats he would know that there would be a welcome for him. The best sermon is an example of a fulfilled, cheerful, loving life. Many of us would do far better to live a sermon than to drag our children against their wishes to go hear one.

If your child has built a wall between you and him, have you forgiven him for the hurt that he has inflicted on you, or is there still animosity there? Do you really want your child to return? Or deep in your heart do you still resent what he did to you?

It is no accident that immediately after talking about God's willingness to give us what we ask for in prayer, Jesus said that we are to forgive others their trespasses against us. (Mark 11:25,26). Wishing is not strong enough in prayer, we must truly desire to the point of knowing inwardly that our request is granted. And there will never be such intense desire where there is resentment and unforgiveness.

The widow who approached the unjust judge would be satisfied only when her desire was fulfilled; she would accept nothing less. That is faith. As James wrote, we must ask with no wavering because the one who wavers is double-minded—he doesn't want his petition wholeheartedly—and such a person will receive nothing of the Lord. (James 1:6-8.)

I've not only experienced God's power to answer my requests with our own three sons, I have seen it with other people.

When I was in Melbourne, Australia, Harold Lawrence, an international director of the Full Gospel Business Mens's Fellowship in that country, came to me after I had told the story of how God brought my three sons home. His wife's name is also Mavis.

"Would you pray with Mavis and me?" he asked. "We are in the same family situation you were in. We have three boys, but we have not seen them or heard from them in a long time."

His boys had been raised in the church but had gone away from the Lord. Neal was attending the university in Melbourne, Mark was a journalist, and Douglas had become a well-known organist. I told Harold and Mavis that I would be happy to pray for their boys.

As I began to pray the Holy Spirit spoke to me.

"The Lord has just told me that your boys will come home," I told them. "In fact, you will hear from them within forty-eight hours."

"That's impossible!" Mavis exclaimed.

"The Bible says in Luke 1:37, 'For with God nothing shall be impossible,'" I reminded her. "Not only will you hear from your boys, you will *see* them within forty-eight hours."

Douglas was probably the finest organist in Melbourne; in 1977 he was elected one of the top thirty organists in the world. The following day he was to give a recital in Melbourne. "This could be the catalyst," I told his mother. "When you see your boys, put your thumbs on their cheeks and the Holy Spirit will come down."

This was on Saturday; on Monday Mavis ran up to me excitedly.

"Wild Bill, you won't believe it! You know when you prayed the other day? Around 10:30 that night the telephone rang. I just knew it was Mark so I answered it by saying, 'Hello, Mark.'

"'Let me talk to Dad, would you please?' he asked.

"Harold picked up the phone and Mark asked him 'How did Mom know it was me? I haven't called in a while.'

"Harold told him, 'Your mom and I have been praying and we just knew it was you.'

"Mark had all kinds of excuses about why he hadn't been to see us, but he said he wanted us to get together again.

"We were planning to go to Douglas' performance on Sunday. Just before we were to leave, the phone rang again. Harold said, 'Mavis, it's for you.' Neal was on the other end of the line.

"'Mom, I don't know why it is, but I'd like to come home for dinner tonight,' he said. 'Douglas is going be in town and I talked to him. Do you think I could come for dinner?'

"We made plans to have dinner together after the performance.

"Mark had arranged to swing by the house to pick us up for Douglas' performance. When he arrrived, I reached up and touched him on the cheeks with my thumbs. Then we went to the church were Douglas was to give his concert—the church with the largest organ in Australia. We met Neal outside and I touched his cheeks also. We walked down the aisle as a family; when Douglas came down the aisle he reached over to kiss me and I touched his cheeks just as you had told me to do.

"Part way through the concert Douglas stopped playing. 'I would like to play some songs that are not on your program,' he announced. He played Felix Mendelssohns's *I Waited for the Lord*, Mozart's *Jesus, Lamb of God, Redeemer*, John Ireland's *Greater Love Hath No Man*, and one or two others including *When the Roll is Called Up Yonder*."

Mavis related how, following the concert, all the boys were in their places at the table where they usually sat. As Harold began to say grace, she looked up and wept, and the Scripture flashed back to her mind, "For with God nothing shall be impossible."

The Bible asks, "Is any thing too hard for the Lord?" (Gen. 18:14). If you have problems with your sons or daughters, turn them over to God and He will care for them. If they have left home like the prodigal, He will bring them back. Stand firm on the promises

He gives you and He will not fail you. Your children will all return from the land of the enemy and your whole household will be saved.

9
Cowboy

All the desk clerk could see was a cowboy hat, a belt buckle and a pair of cowboy boots. It was Cowboy, and he was snoring! I had forgotten him—but God hadn't. The world is full of Cowboys, and it likes to forget they exist. But to God there's no such thing as a bum; they're all precious people, made in His image. It's our job to tell them so.

The bell indicating the end of the workday had just sounded and the govenment workers were streaming out of the state Capitol building in Jackson, Mississippi. Some were running, others were walking—but all were going at breakneck speed.

I waited until they were almost on top of me, then in my usual quiet way I hollered, "Lord!"

Now Peter walked on water, but when those workers heard me holler "Lord!" I beheld an even greater miracle—people started walking on air! Their feet hardly touched the ground. They scattered in all directions trying to get away from me.

I was kneeling on the steps of the Capitol with my arms around a derelict whom I had just met a few minutes earlier. As I led him in the sinner's prayer he experienced a glorious salvation; I could feel the Holy Spirit descend upon him. Let me tell you how I met him.

It was 101 degrees in Jackson that day but the humidity must have been around 300 percent! I was walking down Lamar Street when a drunk staggered by. Slightly larger than I, he was clad in a T-shirt and faded jeans, sported a large eye-catching belt buckle, and wore cowboy boots and a ten-gallon hat. He was all over the place as he walked, staggering so much that he looked as though he was in the middle of the San Francisco earthquake.

The Spirit prompted me to approach him so I sidled up to him and asked, ''How're you doing, Cowboy?''

''How did you know my name?'' he asked, gaping at me in amazement.

''A word of nonsense, I guess,'' I thought to myself. (I like to use all of the gifts in my ministry.) I didn't answer his question, but instead asked him how he was feeling.

''I feel pretty awful,'' he confessed.

''You look terrible,'' I confirmed. ''What happened to you last night?''

''Oh, I really put one on,'' he moaned.

''So did I,'' I said. ''I'm so full of the Spirit, my head . . .''

Before I could finish my sentence he jumped in, ''That's how I feel!''

I could see that he was in desperate need of the Lord so I baited him. ''I've got something right here for you.''

''What is it?'' His eyes brightened.

''It's something you'll really like,'' I enticed.

''Do you carry it with you all the time?''

''I'm never without it. I have a little nip now and then.''

''You do? Where can I get some?''

''Well, the Capitol building is right around the corner,'' I suggested. ''Let's go up on the steps there.''

Cowboy was a little hesitant about going to the Capitol building because everyone would see us there, but I assured him that I didn't mind being seen and he agreed to go with me. So that's how we came to be on the steps of the Capitol when the end-of-the-workday bell sounded.

When we had arrived at the steps Cowboy inquired expectantly, "Okay, where is it?" He was waiting for me to produce the goods.

"Right here," I said, producing my Bible and pointing to it.

"In there?" he asked, a look of incredulity almost causing his eyeballs to pop out of their sockets.

"Yes, it's found in the book of Romans."

Still more puzzled he asked, "Is that an address?"

"The ninth and tenth verses of chapter ten say that if you confess with your mouth the Lord Jesus and believe in your heart that God raised Him from the dead, Cowboy, you can be saved."

"Oh," he sighed, "I don't think that's possible."

When I inquired as to why it wasn't possible for him to be saved, he told me, "Well, I've really been messed up. I've lived here thirteen years and I'm in bad shape. I've done a lot of wrong things."

"Where did you sleep last night?" I asked.

"Oh, I slept in Jackson," he mused.

"Where?" I pressed.

"I slept in a car," he announced, proud of his quick answer.

"Did it have any wheels on it, Cowboy?"

"No, it was in the junk yard."

"And how did you wake up this morning?"

"The cops rousted me out."

I pointed to the Holiday Inn and said proudly,

"See that hotel over there? I'm staying on the fifteenth floor, the very top."

"You are?" he responded enviously.

"Sure, I stay there every night. Cowboy, I used to be like you." That he found hard to believe, pointing out that I was wearing a suit and tie—how could I have ever been like him? I explained that the only difference between him and me was that he was still sitting on a bar stool while I was on the throne of God.

"See, I don't drink that rotgut anymore, I drink Living Water. I don't drink the fruit of the vine, I drink the fruit of the Spirit," I told him.

By now he was excited. "Wow, that sounds pretty good!" he exclaimed. Then the sadness returned to his eyes as he bemoaned, "But you haven't done the things I've done."

I told him how often I had awakened in my car with the sun coming up over the horizon and the only way I could find out what city I was in was to ask some gas station attendant. I related how I awoke one morning and picked up the phone to ask the operator where I was. When she spoke in French I thought, "Oh my, I'm in Paris!" (I wasn't, I was in Montreal.) I told him of the many occasions I had had to have my stomach pumped, how I had often spent the night in the drunk tank and been awakened in the morning with a fire hose.

"You used to do those things?" Cowboy asked, his forehead wrinkled and his eyes as big as saucers. I told him that I had done those things and a lot more, much of which I couldn't remember any longer because the Lord has healed most of my memories.

"Oh, you were rotten!" he confirmed.

"No, I wasn't rotten," I said whimsically, "just

over ripe.''

You see, deep down, every human being is a precious individual created in the image of God. But we've become messed up, just like Cowboy. No one is worthless; no one is a write-off. We are all beautiful people who have been tainted by sin. There is no such thing as a bum; we are all the handiwork of God. It's just that some of us have been perverted by the devil. Because of the Fall we have forgotten that we are the offspring of God and have acted as if we were trash. Blinded by sin, we are ignorant of our true value.

''How do I forget that stuff in my own life?'' Cowboy asked.

''You have to kneel,'' I told him. He wondered why—what difference it made. I told him that when I found the Lord it was on top of a church roof and I had knelt down.

''The preacher put his arms around me and I received salvation, so you have to kneel,'' I told him.

''But we're at the Capitol building!'' he protested.

''Good, this is the best place for it. Just kneel.'' He must have figured that he had very little to lose, so he knelt. When we had finished the sinner's prayer he began to weep.

''Wild Bill, I ain't never cried,'' he said. ''In the thirteen years I've been here, I don't ever remember crying.''

''Cowboy, when I was a drunk I never cried, just like you. My dad and mom were drunks, my sister and my relatives were drunks. I went through a lot of hurts, but I never cried. But since I received the baptism of the Holy Spirit I cry every time the dog gets sick... and Cowboy, we don't have a dog.''

I reached into my coat pocket and pulled out a

ticket for the Full Gospel Business Men's dinner that was to be held that night in the Holiday Inn. "Would you like to eat in the hotel tonight?" I asked, as I offered it to him.

"Sure, I've never been in there before. Who's going to speak?"

"Never mind," I said, "you're going to get a free meal, aren't you?"

"Yeah, but I want to know who's going to speak," he persisted.

"The best speaker in the whole organization," I replied evasively.

"Well, who's that?"

"Me, of course! Who did you think was speaking?"

That evening I was sitting near the front waiting to speak. I knew the instant Cowboy entered because I could smell him. (He was wearing that famous "Jungle Gym" cologne.) And wouldn't you know? There was a seat vacant right down front, and he found it! He was wearing his brown T-shirt that had once been white, his gawdy belt buckle and his cowboy hat. I also noticed that he was displaying a very trend-setting "no-teeth" look. He staggered up to me (this time full of the Holy Spirit) and said loudly, "Hi, Wild Bill! How ya doin', ol' buddy? Gonna speak tonite?" Everyone was looking at me and wondering who this fellow was. "This here's Wild Bill, he's my frien', and he's gonna speak tonite," he began informing those around him.

I spoke, and he was a good audience. He smiled when he was supposed to and clapped at all the right times. I thoroughly enjoyed him. After it was over I said to him, "Cowboy, I'll meet you in the lobby; I have some people to talk to." He nodded agreeably and headed out toward the lobby to wait for me.

In the course of meeting and greeting people after the close of the service, I learned that there was to be a reception held nearby at which the mayor and several other V.I.P.'s were to be present. Would I like to join them? Of course, I would like to join them! The flesh hooked me before I knew what had happened. All thought of Cowboy left my mind. After all, the mayor was important—Cowboy wasn't.

When I opened my room door after the reception the red message light was blinking at me through the darkness. A telephone call. I picked up the receiver and announced, "This is Wild Bill."

"Finally!" the voice on the other end said. "This is the front desk. There's somebody waiting for you down here."

I couldn't think of who would be wanting to see me at that time of night. "Well, who is it?" I asked.

"All I can see is a cowboy hat, a belt buckle, and a pair of cowboy boots . . .and he's snoring! You'd better come down."

"Oh, it's Cowboy!" I exclaimed. "I forgot about him!"

When I reached the lobby I said, "Cowboy, will you forgive me? I didn't mean to do that."

"That's okay, Wild Bill, I needed the sleep," he reassured me. "Let's go witness!"

Our first stop was the bar in the Holiday Inn; it was called the Boll Weevil Room. I never have difficulty finding a stool when I go into a bar. I take my big black Bible and step up to the bar, and instantly I have two stools, one on either side of me. It's like parting the Red Sea.

"Bartender, I'd like a Holy Spirit cocktail," I said.

He disappeared to look at a book. When he came back he said, ''Sir, I'm sorry but I don't know how to mix that.''

''It's very simple,'' I informed him. ''You drop two ice cubes in a glass of water.''

He protested that he couldn't give me a drink of water because the bar wouldn't make any money, so I told him that I knew the owner of the hotel and that I had invited him to speak at our convention. In a flash he made an about-face and got busy mixing my drink.

Cowboy wanted me to show him how to witness. I took my Bible and went over to a lady who was sitting in the corner. When I discovered that she was talking to the wallpaper I left her alone. Cowboy began talking to another woman, but she didn't say a word.

Now ordinarily I talk to drunks even when they are out for the count because I believe their spirit is able to receive from me, even if they are not conscious. A lady who had had a stroke once told me that even when she was lying in a bed on a life-support system she could hear in her spirit what was being said in the room. People would come in and say things like, ''Oh, isn't it a shame for such a beautiful woman to die so young. I wonder if her husband is going to remarry, and who will take care of the children?'' All the time in her spirit that lady was saying to herself, ''I'm not dead, I'm not dead.'' An elderly man went to her hospital room each day and read aloud to her from the book of Romans, and she was completely healed. So from that testimony I learned to give people the Gospel, even though they may seem to be totally incapable of receiving it. I always remember that ''faith cometh by hearing, and hearing by the word of God'' (Rom. 10:17).

So Cowboy and I witnessed in that bar for awhile. Later on Cowboy said, "Let's go to some of my friends. I have a burden for the least, the lost and the last." (He had picked that up from my message that evening.) So we went out to various bars and talked to some of Cowboy's friends. We also went to a couple of "shooting galleries." Now if you have never had any dealings with the drug culture, you probably don't know what a "shooting gallery" is. It is not what you might think. It is a place where drug addicts go to lie on urine-stained mattresses and shoot dope into their arms. These were the people Cowboy played with, stayed with, loved and laughed with. One little girl of thirteen was trying to shoot dope into her arm, but she was in such a terrible mess that she couldn't find the vein.

By about six o'clock the next morning we had covered the whole town. It was beginning to rain, so Cowboy said, "Wild Bill, let's go back to the hotel; I think we've got them all. You got two beds in your room?"

When we arrived at the hotel we walked in the door and I got half-way across the foyer when I realized that Cowboy wasn't with me. I turned around and there he was witnessing to the doorman. I felt like a backslider!

"Why don't you go see if you've got any mail at the desk," he suggested before we went up to the room. I could see my room number behind the desk and the red message light wasn't on. But Cowboy insisted that I check anyway. Next moment, he was talking to the desk clerk. "Do you know Jesus?" he asked her forthrightly.

"No, I don't."

"Would you like to know Him?" Then and there he led her to the Lord while I, the evangelist, stood by with egg all over my face.

When we finally reached my room I turned on the air conditioner because by that time Cowboy was really rancid. I suggested that he might like to take a shower, an idea he fairly jumped at. I turned on the water for him. While he showered he sang the one song I had taught him, "Jesus Loves Me, This I Know."

"Be quiet," I urged as discreetly as I could because it was still very early in the morning.

"Listen, if anybody knocks on the door, you answer it and tell them, 'Jesus loves you'; that'll get rid of 'em," Cowboy answered.

When he had finished showering I offered him some of my clean underwear but he declined. Then the Lord spoke to me: "Wild Bill, I want you to give Cowboy a suit."

That was fine with me. I told Cowboy that the Lord wanted me to give him a suit. I took down a good looking brown suit that Mavis had packed for me.

"I don't want that one," Cowboy said.

"You're picky, aren't you?" I said. "Here's a nice gray suit."

"I don't want that one either." Cowboy wasn't about to let me palm off any of my old suits on him. He pointed to another suit that was brand new, still wrapped in the cellophane. "I want that blue one."

Now if there was one suit I didn't want to give away it was my beautiful new blue suit. My friend Chuck Donato had bought it for me. I thought back to the day he said to me, "Wild Bill, the Lord just told me to buy you a suit."

"That's right, Chuck, the Lord's speaking to you.

Listen to Him.''

"He said that I am to buy you a suit as soon as we get home from this trip," Chuck continued. I suggested that we change our reservations and fly home together: I didn't want him to develop buyer's remorse, I needed that suit. So we went to the store together and Chuck asked me what kind of suit I wanted. Well, for me there was only one kind of suit to buy, a blue one.

"I've got some brown suits and some gray suits," I told him, "but Mavis picked those out for me and I hide them because I don't like them. I want a blue suit, one that matches my eyes."

Chuck tried to steer me over to the $19 suits but I wasn't going to be put off. "Here it is, Chuck," I announced triumphantly when my eye latched onto the one I wanted. "It does match my eyes, doesn't it, Chuck?" He agreed that it was a nice suit so I hinted that a tie and a shirt would look good with it.

Soon after that I left for Jackson, so I took my beautiful new suit with me. And now here I was faced with Cowboy who was determined to have *my* suit.

"Oh no, you can't have that one, I haven't worn it yet," I told him.

At that point a little tear appeared in Cowboy's eye and rolled down his cheek. "Wild Bill, I ain't never had a new suit," he said sadly.

"Cowboy, I ain't hardly ever had a new suit either."

"Well, if you don't want me to have it . . ."

"I didn't say I don't want you to have it. Okay, try it on; but if it won't fit, it won't fit."

We took the suit out of its cellophane wrapper and off its hanger and Cowboy tried it on. Other than the vest being a little snug, the suit fit Cowboy like a glove! In fact, it looked as though it had been tailor made for him.

"Gee, I really like this suit," he announced proudly. I really liked it too, but I knew that the Lord wanted Cowboy to have it.

"Wild Bill, I have a burden," he suddenly said, changing the subject. "My mom and dad don't know Jesus."

"That's a good burden to have, Cowboy," I assured him.

"Trouble is, I can't get back to Ada to talk to 'em about Him," he said.

When I inquired as to where Ada might be, Cowboy explained, "You take the bus and get off at Oklahoma City, then you take another bus—it's a long way to go."

When I asked him if he had any idea where he might get the money for his ticket, Cowboy suggested, "Well, I was hopin' maybe you'd let me have it."

I hadn't been on a bus in a long time, being a jet traveler. The last time I was on a bus it only cost $1.50 to go from Anaheim to Newport Beach. At the bus depot the Greyhound man told us that Cowboy's ticket would cost $47.67. "I don't want to buy your bus or stock in your company," I responded, "I just want a one-way ticket to Ada, Oklahoma."

It was beginning to rain so I hurried Cowboy onto the bus. "You'd better get in there quick or the blue suit will get all wet," I urged.

At that moment the Lord spoke to me again. "Wild Bill, do you love Me?"

"Lord, I love You."

"Then feed My sheep."

"Lord, it's eight o'clock in the morning and I haven't slept in twenty-four hours, so run that one past me once more, slowly."

"Feed My sheep," the Lord repeated, going on to explain, "Cowboy is going back to Oklahoma and he hasn't got any money. The last meal he had was with you and he's going to be hungry."

"That's the last meal I had too," I protested, "and if I give him all my money then I'm going to be hungry too."

Then the Lord delivered one that was not fair. "Have I ever left you or forsaken you?" He asked. What could I say? I reached into my pocket and gave Cowboy my money, telling him that it was to buy some food on his journey home.

Cowboy was standing on the steps of the bus with his arm hanging out. By now it was raining heavily. He began to weep. "Wild Bill, I ain't been a Christian very long," he sobbed. "You gave me a suit and you don't even know me. You gave me the money to buy my bus ticket, and you gave me money to buy some food. If this is what it's like being a Christian then I'm sure glad I became one. Praise God, glory, hallelujah!" (He was a quick learner; he had all the words down pat.)

I was deeply touched that Cowboy thought of me as a giving person because before I had come to know the Lord my life was totally selfish. In those days I lived only to get.

"Cowboy, get your elbow back in there," I insisted as the rain came down still harder. With that the bus revved up its engine, turned around, and pulled away from the terminal. I watched it disappear down Lamar Street. The last thing I saw of Cowboy was that blue elbow sticking out the window in the rain again.

I have a nosey wife who likes to unpack my clothes when I get home to see what I gave away, and whether I used two handkerchiefs instead of one. So as soon as I got back I rushed into the house and unpacked by bag in a hurry so she wouldn't discover that my blue suit was missing.

The first question Mavis asked me was, "How did the suit look, honey?"

"It looked beautiful." (I wasn't lying; it did look beautiful—just not on me.)

"Did you like it?"

"I loved it." (True again. I loved it when it came into my life, and I loved it when it left!)

I didn't tell Mavis about Cowboy nor how I had given my suit away.

Four months later, my secretary came into my office with a large bag wrapped in butcher paper and bearing my name and address on the outside. "Here's something that came in the mail for you, Wild Bill," she announced. I opened the bag and inside was the blue suit, with the vest, shirt, and tie. The vest was a little torn in the back because Cowboy was broader than I was. I told Mavis the story of how I had given it away, but I couldn't figure out how it had come to be returned to me.

I was leaving for Tulsa, Oklahoma, and was to be gone six days. While there my ear began to hurt. On my way home our plane touched down in Oklahoma City. John Wales, a brother in the Capistrano Valley Chapter of the Full Gospel Business Men's Fellowship and an ex-airline pilot, was on the plane, so I mentioned that my ear was really hurting. Just as Jonathan reached out to David and strengthened him, John reached over and touched me. I believe he may well have saved my life that day.

When I got back to Anaheim, I went in for a medical examination. I was hospitalized immediately. At first the doctors thought I had a brain tumor. Upon closer examination, however, I was diagnosed as having encephalitis of the brain stem, together with Hamsey-Hunt syndrome, and the prognosis was not good. I was in excruciating pain. The nerves on the right side of my brain were inflamed, causing me to have quadruple vision in my right eye and complete loss of hearing in my right ear. The entire right side of my face had collapsed some two and a half inches so that I now looked like Charles Laughton in *The Hunchback of Notre Dame.*

There were two things I was skeptical of when I became a charismatic. The first was the supernatural filling of teeth. One lady told me that the Lord had given her five gold crowns. "Fine," I thought to myself, "but I would like to have seen it happen."

The second thing I was skeptical of was out-of-body experiences. While I was in the hospital I had one of those experiences.

I was in terrible pain one day, when suddenly I found myself looking down on my own face. It looked awful, contorted in agony. Then in the next moment I found myself on a hill looking down on a large mansion with thousands and thousands of people in the front yard. I realized that I was in heaven and that the mansion was mine. I turned to the Lord and asked Him, "What are all these people doing in my front yard?''

''These are the people you have individually led to salvation,'' He answered. I looked at some of them.

There was my cousin Doug. When I visited him in the hospital, he had been dying of cancer, surviving only on life-support systems. The nurses tried to throw me out, but I insisted that Doug come to know Jesus before he died. He got down on his knees and asked the Lord into his heart.

I saw three Eskimos and I recognized them as some I had led to the Lord while I was in Alaska. There had been fourteen of them outside the mission in Anchorage, blue with cold, clad in T-shirts. All of them were drunk, and when one fell down in the snow I had picked him up. I tried to take them into the mission but the people there wouldn't allow it. They told me that there was a rule forbidding drunks to come in.

''That's a dumb rule,'' I objected. ''How do you expect to ever sober them up if you don't let them in?''

When I got nowhere, I said, ''Follow me, guys.'' We went across the street to a McDonald's restaurant where I bought them each a cup of coffee and watched the fourteen of them turn from blue to brown.

In front of that mansion I saw a couple of other Eskimos I had led to the Lord while in Fairbanks. Up there, some of the Eskimos walk across the frozen Cheena River to save themselves a couple of miles on their long trek home. Sometimes in the spring when the thaw begins they fall through and drown. No one knows where they are until the ice has melted; there have been as many as fifteen or twenty bodies found in that icy water.

On that lawn were people from all over the world whom I had led to the Lord. I recognized a man from

Yugoslavia whom I had baptized the night the police arrived just after we had finished baptizing.

I also recognized a lady whom I had met in a hotel elevator in New Orleans. On that occasion Demos Shakarian, Founder and President of the Full Gospel Business Men's Fellowship International, was in the elevator with me. Normally when a person goes into an elevator he will watch the numbers on the floor indicator; but I'm different. I always watch the people in the car with me.

Demos and I had entered the elevator on the thirty-seventh floor and had started down to the lobby. When the car stopped on the thirty-sixth floor, a woman got in with a glass full of booze in her hand. She was wearing a name tag and was obviously coming from an all-night party, while we were on our way down to breakfast. Her name tag read, "Ruth Jones from Connecticut."

I said, "You're Ruth Jones from Connecticut."

"How'd you know my name?"

"Everybody knows Ruth Jones from Connecticut."

After a while, we reached the lobby and Demos stepped out of the elevator, but I didn't follow him. Instead, I hit the button for the top floor. There were forty floors in that hotel and on the way up I told Ruth my testimony about having been a drunk. At that instant, for the first time in her life she was able to admit that she was a drunk!

When we reached the fortieth floor I pressed the button for the lobby and began to lead her in the sinner's prayer. When we arrived at the lobby the doors opened to reveal a puzzled Demos, who had been waiting for me.

"Meet Ruth Jones, a new sister from Connecticut!" I said.

Remembering the pain I was suffering in my body, I said, "Lord, I don't want to go back. I want to stay here."

The Lord said, "Wild Bill, look at one last person in the left-hand corner." I looked, and there was a big man wearing a cowboy hat, cowboy boots, a large belt buckle, a blue suit, and he had all his teeth too!

"That's Cowboy, Lord!" I exclaimed. "What happened?"

Then, as if I were watching a movie in slow motion I was back at the bus station on Lamar Street. The bus disappeared down the street, and then I found myself in Ada, Oklahoma, where Cowboy got off the bus. He walked to the home of his eighty-year-old mom and dad and led them to the Lord. He took them to the church to pray at the altar. Each night I watched him go down to the bars where he found backsliders and sinners and took them over to the local Full-Gospel church. He did that night after night.

Then one night while he was witnessing to some of his former friends on the street, a truck came by and struck Cowboy. He was dead before he hit the ground. At the mortuary they dressed him in his blue suit, and the preacher at the little church held a service.

"How many in this room are here as a result of Cowboy?" he asked. Out of the two hundred people present, half raised their hands.

"How many are here because of someone who knew Cowboy?" Most of the other half raised their hands. The preacher gave an altar call, and there beside Cowboy's casket fourteen people accepted Jesus!

They were going to cremate Cowboy's body, so they took off his blue suit. As the mortician was going through the pockets he found a card that had my name and address on it, so he wrapped up the suit and sent it to me.

Today, I wear that suit proudly. The smell of formaldehyde has gone now, but the memory of Cowboy is ever fresh. To the world he looked like a bum, but to God he was a very special person. It's winning people like Cowboy to the Lord that makes me want to remain in the flesh a lot longer yet.

There is a poster which reads, "I know I'm somebody, 'cause God don't make no junk!" That's true of every human being on earth, no matter how down-and-out he may appear. In James 2:1-9 we read about a man who came into a meeting dressed in fine clothes and was shown special attention and provided a choice seat, while a poor man in rags was pushed aside and told to sit on the floor. "Listen, my beloved brethren," James challenges us, "did not God choose the poor of this world to be rich in faith and heirs of the kingdom which He promised to those who love Him?" (v. 5 NAS).

There are a great many Cowboys in the world, waiting for someone who cares enough to bring them into their inheritance. They are potential kings dressed in beggar's rags. They are all around us, every day of our lives, no matter where we live or work. Don't you want to help me bring them into the Kingdom? And with them, hundreds and thousands of others who will come to Jesus through their testimony?

Cowboy has gone, but I pray that his message will live on in the hearts of all who read this story so that countless precious souls can join him with his Savior in heaven for all eternity.

Epilogue

There are a lot of lonely people in this world, people whose lives are empty and who deperately long for a reason for living. Even though I was partying it up on my ascent to success, deep down inside I was one of those lonely people.

When Jesus came into my life the restless striving to prove that I was somebody ended. For the first time in my life I *knew* that I was somebody! He gave me a reason for living and days that are packed with excitement.

I'm looking forward to that day when my earthly life is over and I go walking into the front yard of my heavenly mansion where a lot of people, some of whom I've talked about in this book, are waiting for me. We're going to rejoice and have a wonderful time together. I would like to see you there with us one day too.

If you're tired of emptiness, Jesus wants to make your life meaningful. If you're sick of loneliness, He wants to welcome you into His family. If you've had enough of inner turmoil, He wants to give you a sense of peace and fulfillment.

All you have to do is confess with your mouth the Lord Jesus and believe in your heart, and you will enter into a whole new dimension of life. The limitless love of God waits to enfold you and to transform you into the beautiful person you were created to be.

If you would like to accept Jesus into your life, pray this simple prayer out loud:

Dear Lord Jesus, I believe that You are the Son of God and that God has raised You from the dead. I ask You to come into my heart right now and save

me by Your grace.

Thank You, Lord, for saving me. Now I am a Christian. Now I will serve You for the rest of my life and will spend eternity in heaven with You.

Amen.

If you prayed this prayer in sincerity, then you are saved, born again, a new creature—a Christian! Why not sign your name in this book, just as I put mine on that church wall the day Jesus saved me. Then write me at the address below and tell me about your decision. I would like to rejoice with you and to be your friend.

God bless you!

Today, I, the undersigned, accepted Jesus Christ as my personal Savior and Lord.

Signature: *Ludwig Jagi Machek* RE-DEDICATED

Date: DECEMBER 5/1980

Address all correspondence to:
Bill Monteith
1958 Woodworth Road
Anaheim, CA 92804

About the Author

A man aflame with the love of God, Bill Monteith has a dynamic testimony of how the Lord delivered him from drunkenness when he gave his heart and life to Jesus Christ.

Bill is Fellowship Group Manager at the world laymens' headquarters of the Full Gospel Business Men's Fellowship International in Costa Mesa, California. His responsibilities include the Chapter Department, Conventions, Global Outreach, Prison Ministry, Special Projects and the Annual World Convention.

A graduate of the University of Southern California, Bill held executive positions with a large construction and financial corporation and two title insurance companies. He now travels the globe telling how only God can build a new life on a solid Rock, give the title deed to eternal life, and repair a broken heart and home.

A devoted husband of 33 years, father and grandfather, Bill and his lovely wife Mavis live in Anaheim, California. They have dedicated their lives to telling others of the saving, delivering, healing and restorative power of Jesus Christ.

For additional copies of *Wild Bill,* write:

PRAISE BOOKS
P. O. Box 35035
Tulsa, OK 74153

.